CHARLES A. LINDBERGH

A HUMAN HERO

CHARLES A. LINDBERGH

A HUMAN HERO

James Cross Giblin

CLARION BOOKS
New York

Clarion Books
a Houghton Mifflin Company imprint
215 Park Avenue South, New York, NY 10003
Text copyright © 1997 by James Cross Giblin

Text is 13.25 / 16.25-point Dante Roman
Book design by Carol Goldenberg

Library of Congress Cataloging-in-Publication Data

Giblin, James.
Charles A. Lindbergh : a human hero / by James Cross Giblin.
p.   cm.
Includes bibliographical references and index.
Summary: A biography of the pilot whose life was full of controversy and tragedy,
but also fulfilling achievements.
ISBN: 0-395-63389-3
1. Lindbergh, Charles A. (Charles Augustus), 1902–1974—Juvenile literature.
2. Air pilots—United States—Biography—Juvenile literature.
[1. Lindbergh, Charles A. (Charles Augustus), 1902–1974. 2. Air pilots.] I. Title.
TL540.L5G53   1997
629.13'092—dc20   [B] 96-9501
CIP   AC

KPT 10 9 8 7 6 5 4 3 2

Frontispiece: *His shy boyishness is apparent in this photo of Charles.* Library of Congress.

Once again for DAVIDA LIST,
with many thanks

Acknowledgments

For their help with this project, I want to thank the following individuals and institutions: Sue Alexander; *American Heritage*; Marion Dane Bauer; Doe Boyle; Dorothy Briley; Norman Currie, Corbis-Bettman; Barbara Elleman; the Library of Congress; the Minnesota Historical Society; the Missouri Historical Society; Jim Murphy; the National Air and Space Museum, Smithsonian Institution; the New York Public Library; John Orlock; Jane Resh Thomas.

Of particular help was my visit to the Charles A. Lindbergh House and History Center in Little Falls, Minnesota. As I wandered through the house, I felt as if I were stepping back in time to the long-ago summers Charles Lindbergh spent there as a boy. It gave me a clearer sense of the man, and of the world from which he sprang.

—J.C.G.

Contents

Charles A. Lindbergh

A Human Hero

The Spirit of St. Louis hangs at center left in the Milestones of Aviation gallery of the National Air and Space Museum in Washington. Below it, at bottom right, is the first plane the Wright Brothers flew. National Air and Space Museum, Smithsonian Institution.

Such a Small Plane

They're all there in the central hall of the National Air and Space Museum in Washington, D.C. The 1903 Flyer in which the Wright brothers made the first successful heavier-than-air flight. The 1962 Mercury spacecraft in which John Glenn became the first American to orbit the earth. And the Apollo 11 command module that carried Neil Armstrong, Edwin Aldrin Jr., and Michael Collins to the moon and back in July 1969.

Above them all, hanging from the ceiling on wires, is what looks at first glance like just another old, small plane. It is only twenty-seven-and-a-half feet long and nine feet ten inches high, with a wingspan of just forty-six feet. The cockpit is tiny and doesn't even have a front window.

Then a visitor notices the name painted on the nose and realizes why this plane occupies such a prominent spot in the Air and Space Museum. For it is the *Spirit of St. Louis*, the plane in which Charles A. Lindbergh, in May 1927, made the first nonstop flight from the United States to Europe.

Lindbergh's flight scored more than one first. Not only did he fly the 3,600-mile distance from New York to Paris without landing anywhere along the route, but he made the long journey alone. This heroic feat transformed the twenty-five-year-old pilot into an instant celebrity. Before the flight few people beyond his family, friends, and coworkers had ever heard of Charles Lindbergh. After it he could not go anywhere without being surrounded by an admiring crowd.

Today celebrities are common in every field, from politics to sports to popular music. Some are heroes like Lindbergh, others notorious criminals. The media, especially television, can create such celebrities overnight and discard them just as quickly. In the process hundreds if not thousands of individuals are given what the artist Andy Warhol once called their "fifteen minutes of fame."

Charles Lindbergh was one of the first celebrities to be created by this kind of media buildup. Although there was no television in his day, many families listened to late-breaking news on their radios, which were marketed for the first time in the 1920s. Millions also saw firsthand reports of what was going on in the world in the newsreels that were shown then with every movie. And newspapers made use of the latest advances in radio, photography, and transportation to bring their readers up-to-the-minute coverage of events like Lindbergh's Paris flight.

The ceaseless media attention that Lindbergh received would change his life forever. It also changed the attitudes of people everywhere toward celebrities like him. No longer were they remote figures standing above the crowd. Instead, thanks to radio broadcasts and movie newsreels, people felt as close to their heroes as they did to the man or woman next door. They could hear their voices, see their faces, follow them into their workplaces and even their living rooms. The person's privacy might be sacrificed along the way. But wasn't that the price modern celebrities had to pay in exchange for fame?

Maybe most famous people were willing to pay it, but not Charles Lindbergh. He had always been an unusually private person—a loner—and he wasn't about to change his ways to satisfy the demands of the media. The press hadn't helped him to achieve his dream of flying nonstop to Paris. He had done that almost entirely on his own. And his dream hadn't been inspired by any radio broadcast or newsreel. It had started back when he was a boy, spending his summers on the banks of the Upper Mississippi River in Minnesota.

✦ CHAPTER ONE ✦

A Driver at Eleven

One afternoon in 1913 Charles Lindbergh was playing upstairs in his family's summer home in Little Falls, Minnesota, when he heard the sound of an engine in the distance. He thought it must be an automobile, and went on sorting the stones he and his mother had collected from the creek bed.

Suddenly he stopped and listened again. No automobile engine made that kind of sound, and it was on the wrong side of the house—the side that faced the river. Curious, he went to the window and looked out. He couldn't see anything, but the roar was louder now, and it seemed to be coming from the sky.

Could it be an airplane? The year before, Charles had seen one for the first time when his mother took him to a flying exhibition in Fort Myer, Virginia. He had watched, enthralled, as the pilot gave a bombing demonstration by dropping oranges on the outline of a battleship that was traced on the ground. Now maybe an airplane was right here in Minnesota, and about to fly over his house.

Not wanting to miss a thing, Charles opened the window and climbed up the sloping roof of the house to its peak. From there he had a good view of the Mississippi River, flowing languidly past the Lindbergh place. And in the sky, coming ever closer, he saw the plane.

It was a biplane, and not much more advanced than the craft in which the Wright brothers had made their famous flight a few years earlier. The pilot perched precariously at the forward end of an open-sided box whose top and bottom were held together by a network of wires. Other wires and braces attached the box to the plane's double wings.

Charles watched the plane until it disappeared from view upriver. Then he rushed downstairs to tell his mother about it. Oh, yes, she said, there had been a story in the local paper. An aviator had come to town and was taking passengers up for rides. But the rides were very expensive, and dangerous, too. What if the engine stopped, or a wing fell off?

Charles would have liked to go up for a ride, but he knew better than to suggest it to his mother. Still, he could imagine soaring above the river like the pilot he'd seen, and looking down on rapids, logjams, and foaming waterfalls. . . .

Charles and his mother lived a divided life. Half the year they spent at the house and farm in Little Falls, which Charles loved. The other half they lived in rented hotel suites and furnished apartments in Washington, D.C., where Charles's father—whose name was also Charles Augustus Lindbergh—served in the House of Representatives.

Young Charles thoroughly disliked Washington. "For me," Lindbergh wrote later, "the city formed a prison. Red brick houses replaced the woodlands on our farm. . . . It was the clank of streetcars, not the hoot of an owl, that woke me at night."

Charles's life was divided in another way. His parents separated when Charles was five, and from then on he lived with his mother. The Lindberghs did not divorce, however; that would have meant the end of the elder Lindbergh's political career. The God-fearing Minnesota farmers of the early 1900s who had sent him to Congress would never elect a divorced man to represent them.

Politics seemed to run in the Lindbergh family. Charles's father, Charles Senior, had been born in Sweden, where *his* father, August, served in the country's Riksdag, or Parliament. Disgusted with Sweden's rigid class structure, August decided in 1859 to leave his native

Charles Lindbergh at age six with his mother, Evangeline. National Air and Space Museum, Smithsonian Institution.

Evangeline Lindbergh with the infant Charles. Photo by Nelson, Little Falls, the Minnesota Historical Society.

land and immigrate with his family to America. They settled on a small farm in central Minnesota near other immigrants from Sweden and Germany.

Charles Senior—known to his friends as C.A.—dropped out of school at age ten to help his family run the farm. He returned to school at twenty to make up the years he had lost, then went on to study law at the University of Michigan. After getting his degree, C.A. established a successful law practice in the town of Little Falls and wed Mary LaFond, the daughter of a family with whom he had boarded.

C.A. and Mary Lindbergh had two daughters, Lillian and Eva, and everything seemed to be going smoothly for the young family. Then Mary died unexpectedly following a minor operation. The grief-stricken C.A. moved into a hotel in Little Falls, and his mother took over the care of his two daughters. Not long afterward C.A. met another boarder at the hotel, Evangeline Land, the new science teacher at Little Falls High School.

Evangeline was an unusual young woman for her time. Not only had she gone to college, but she had studied science, earning a B.A. in chemistry from the University of Michigan. She was also attractive, with curly brown hair and large, expressive blue eyes. C.A. found himself wanting to spend more and more time with her.

Evangeline responded just as strongly to C.A. He might be forty-one—seventeen years older than she—but he was still a remarkably handsome man, as well as the most prominent attorney in Little Falls. They were married in March 1901, just seven months after they met. And their only child, Charles, was born less than a year later, on February 4, 1902.

In 1906 C.A.'s friends persuaded him to run for Congress as a progressive Republican. C.A. had always believed that farmers like his father were treated unfairly by bankers who demanded high interest rates for loans, and by railroad owners who charged exorbitant fees to ship their crops. He promised to fight for the farmers' interests if sent to Congress, and he won by a sizable majority.

Evangeline supported C.A.'s political ambitions and looked forward to the move to Washington. She thought living there would provide more social and cultural opportunities for everyone in the family—C.A., herself, and little Charles. C.A.'s two daughters had decided to stay behind with relatives in Minnesota. But within a year of their going to Washington, Evangeline and C.A. separated. Why?

Much later Charles told a biographer of his father that it was a "tragic case" of two people who, though deeply in love, were unable to live together.

On C.A.'s side, the problem may have been his reticence. He was always outspoken on political issues, but he had a hard time expressing his personal feelings. As he once wrote his daughter Eva, "The trouble with me is I don't tell people when I am pleased. . . ."

Evangeline usually kept her emotions under a tight rein also. So her separation from C.A. may have come about simply because neither of them could communicate openly and freely with the other. Fortunately for Charles, his parents remained on friendly terms. As a consequence, although he lived with his mother, he was able to spend a good deal of time with his father.

When he was growing up, Charles's year followed a basic pattern. After a summer in Little Falls, he and Evangeline would take the train to Detroit for a two-week visit with Charles's maternal grandparents. Then he and his mother traveled on by train to Washington, where they spent the winter. In the spring the two of them stopped off in Detroit for another visit before returning home to Little Falls.

Charles looked forward to the weeks spent with his grandparents. His grandfather, Dr. Charles H. Land, was both a dentist and an inventor. He perfected a method of making porcelain crowns for decayed teeth that was used everywhere until plastic crowns were developed in the 1940s. Dr. Land also invented a self-rocking cradle and an air-filtration system to keep Detroit's pollution out of his home.

From the time Charles was a small boy, Dr. Land encouraged his natural curiosity. He took his grandson for long walks in the woods and taught him how to recognize the various birds, wildflowers, and mush-rooms. In Dr. Land's basement laboratory Charles learned how to make molds, cast metal, and work with electricity.

In Washington Charles often got bored listening to his father give long political speeches filled with big words and vague ideas. He much preferred the clear, precise language of science that Grandfather Land used when he was explaining something. From then on Charles always tried to employ a scientific approach himself, relying on facts, not emotions, when confronted with a new problem.

The summers at the house in Little Falls were filled with fun, work, and challenges for Charles. His father lived in an apartment in Minneapolis during the summer months, but he often came to Little Falls for a visit. He and Charles would take their rifles—Charles had gotten his first gun when he was six—and go hunting together in the nearby woods or on the shores of a lake. Following a rule of C.A.'s, they never shot at birds unless they were in flight.

In 1912 C.A. bought the Lindberghs' first car, a Model-T Ford that Mrs. Lindbergh christened Maria. The car had a four-cylinder engine, carbide headlights, a folding waterproof cloth top, and side curtains that could be attached on rainy days.

A year later, when he was just eleven, Charles learned to drive Maria and soon became more comfortable behind the wheel than either of his parents. On nice days he and his mother would take a spin to a nearby town or lake and have a picnic. Charles never ran into any trouble with the police. In 1913 automobiles were rare and driving rules virtually nonexistent. So no one got particularly upset if they saw an eleven-year-old boy at the wheel of a car.

Charles had much more difficulty with the hazards that all drivers faced then: unpaved roads that turned to mud after a heavy rain and temperamental engines that refused to start no matter how many times you cranked them. But Charles had made a scientific study of combustion engines, and he prided himself on knowing how to get Maria started and keep her going.

Charles at ten with his politician father, C. A. Lindbergh. Minnesota Historical
Society.

C.A. enlisted Charles as his driver when he traveled around his election district, meeting voters and campaigning. While C.A. gave speeches denouncing New York City bankers and what he called the "money trust," Charles could usually be found beside Maria, making notes in the logbook he kept about the car's performance.

The elder Lindbergh believed in giving young people independence and letting them make their own decisions. "The more childlife is dominated," he once wrote, "the easier adults are influenced. They become accustomed to having others direct them and do not think for themselves."

C.A. practiced what he preached with his son, Charles. Once when the two of them were on a campaign trip to Duluth, he let Charles drive down the steep hill on which the northern Minnesota city is built. A freight train was crossing the road at the foot of the hill. Charles put on the brakes to slow the car—but they failed to take hold.

Charles glanced quickly at his father, but C.A. said nothing and made no move to help his son. Left on his own, Charles did the only thing possible to avoid crashing into the slow-moving train. He swerved the car into a ditch at the side of the road so skillfully that neither he nor his father was injured, though the car was badly damaged.

"It was a good chance to see what sort of stuff the boy was made of," C.A. said later to a friend. "And he came through."

CHAPTER TWO

Cycling Near the Edge

W hen World War I broke out in Europe in 1914, C.A. took a strong stand against it. He opposed any suggestion that the United States side with the Allies, Great Britain and France, in their struggle against the Central Powers, Germany and Austria-Hungary. In Congress he made speeches charging that the "money interests" were promoting U.S. involvement because they hoped to profit from the war.

The Allies had many supporters, not only in Congress but throughout the country, and C.A. was widely criticized for his views. As a result he decided not to run for reelection to Congress in 1916, thinking he would most likely be defeated. He left Washington in March 1917, a month before the United States finally entered the war.

With C.A. no longer in Congress, there was no reason for Charles and his mother to stay in Washington either. They spent the winter of 1917–18 in Little Falls, and Charles enrolled as a senior at Little Falls High School.

By his own account, Charles was not a good student. It would have been surprising if he had been. Between the ages of eight and sixteen he had attended eleven different schools in Washington, Detroit, and Little Falls, and never completed a full semester in any of them. As a senior in Little Falls he got E's (for Excellent) in physics and VG's (for

Very Good) in chemistry and mechanical drawing, but M's (for Medium) in English and history.

Being an only child, and having moved around so much, Charles also found it difficult to socialize and make friends. He didn't take part in any organized sports or other extracurricular activities, and rarely went fishing or hunting with other boys. A fellow senior, Roy Larson, said of Charles, "I guess I knew him as well as anyone, but I never knew him well. He always kept to himself, never mixed it up with the rest of us."

Charles showed no interest in the opposite sex. Bertha Rothwell, another Little Falls classmate, remembered that "he paid no attention to the girls, and the girls paid no attention to him." Never during his high school years did he have a date, apparently. Roy Larson thought this was due to the fact that Charles "was always sort of bashful and would blush every time anyone said anything to him."

But he wasn't bashful where machines were concerned. Ever since the afternoons in Grandfather Land's laboratory, Charles had wanted to learn everything he could about them. Now, in Little Falls, he spent hours in the workshop of Martin Engstrom, a hardware merchant. "Charles was always talking about internal combustion engines," Engstrom said. "Always asking me questions about them."

In 1916 Charles had persuaded his father to buy a tractor for the Little Falls farm. The vehicle was delivered in pieces to the Engstrom store and Charles insisted on assembling it himself, a job that took him three days. "It ran perfectly," Engstrom said later.

Through the Engstrom store Charles also ordered a twin-cylinder Excelsior motorcycle. "I loved its power and speed and soon became a skillful rider," he wrote.

The motorcycle was the one thing that all his classmates at Little Falls High School remembered about Charles. Many of them thought he drove it recklessly, and they were surprised that he never had an accident.

Roy Larson saw firsthand some of the risks that Charles took with his motorcycle. During school vacations Larson worked at the Little Falls

The teenage Charles astride his Excelsior motorcycle. Minnesota Historical Society.

power plant on the bank of the Mississippi River. Around the plant ran a cinder path that slanted from the road in front, went through a thicket of chokeberry bushes, and then hugged the river's edge. At that point the riverbank was quite steep.

Charles always used the path as a shortcut on his way from the Lindbergh farm to town. Roy Larson would see him come roaring down the road on his motorcycle, then cut off with a shrieking skid onto the path through the chokeberries. Once past the bushes, he would hurtle along the riverbank at top speed, sending cinders and clumps of earth spinning into the Mississippi.

"It seemed like he wanted to see how close to the edge he could get without plunging in," Larson recalled later. "Finally the boss got scared and had the path dug out so Charles couldn't go that way anymore."

At a high school assembly in late winter, the principal announced that due to the wartime need for food, any student who wanted to work on a farm could leave school and still receive full credit for his classes. Charles jumped at the opportunity. He took over the management of the family farm, raised cattle, sheep, and chickens, and was still able to graduate with his class in June 1918.

After graduation Charles kept on running the farm while he decided what he wanted to do next. On long autumn evenings, after the feeding and milking were done, he would read books, magazines, and newspapers in the warm kitchen by the light of a kerosene lamp. The Lindberghs had neither electricity nor a telephone on the farm.

Charles read with interest all the news reports from the far-off European war. But he paid special attention to accounts of the battles being fought in the air by brave pilots like the American Eddie Rickenbacker, the Briton Edward ("Mick") Maddock, and the German Ernst Udet. He also waited eagerly for each new installment of a serial magazine story, "Tim o' the Scoots," about a daring Scottish fighter pilot who became an ace.

It was the latter story more than anything else, Lindbergh wrote later, that helped him decide to enlist in the army when he was old enough and become a fighter pilot himself. He had to abandon that dream, though, when word came in November 1918 that an armistice had been signed, ending World War I. The army was no longer interested in training new pilots.

After another year of farming Charles, at his mother's urging, applied for admission to the University of Wisconsin in Madison. It had an excellent department of mechanical engineering, which Charles thought he'd like to major in.

Charles's application was accepted, despite his mediocre high school grades, and he and his mother made plans to move to Madison. She got a job teaching junior high science there and rented an apartment for herself and Charles on the top floor of a three-story house. Charles turned their Little Falls place over to a tenant farmer and rode his

Charles looks through a photo album at the University of Wisconsin. Minnesota Historical Society.

motorcycle to Madison. In September 1920 he enrolled as a freshman at the university.

It wasn't long before Charles became bored with the college routine. He might read one of his textbooks for an hour or so, but then he would go for a hike around the lake, or take a long motorcycle ride through the countryside, or engage in target practice on the university's rifle range.

By early 1922 he was asking himself what he would do with a college degree if he graduated. He didn't want to end up at a desk job in some factory or office building. But what *did* he want to do with his life?

Aviation continued to interest him, and when a college friend, Delos Dudley, wrote away for information about several different flying schools, Charles studied the brochures avidly. He was particularly impressed with one from the Nebraska Aircraft Corporation, located in the state capital, Lincoln. It offered flying instruction as part of its sales promotion efforts, and would give him the opportunity to learn how airplanes were made as well as how to fly them.

When Charles told his father that he wanted to leave the university and sign up with a flying school, C.A. tried to get him to change his mind. The future of aviation might be bright, C.A. said, but the life of an individual pilot was likely to be brief. He cited an article he'd read that claimed the average pilot could expect to fly only nine hundred hours before he suffered a fatal accident.

Nine hundred hours in the air sounded like quite a long time to Charles. And with luck and careful flying, he figured he could have a much longer career than that. He fended off every argument his father put forth, and eventually C.A. gave in.

So did Evangeline, although she hated to see Charles drop out of college and feared that they would never again spend much time together. "But you must lead your own life," she said. "I mustn't hold you back."

Charles was eager to embark on his new life. In late March 1922, without bothering to complete his sophomore year, he left the University of Wisconsin and headed for Lincoln, Nebraska, on his trusty motorcycle.

✧ CHAPTER THREE ✧

Wingwalking

Before Charles walked through the doors of the Nebraska Aircraft Corporation, he had never been close enough to an airplane to touch it. Now here he was, surrounded by the basic parts that made up a plane. His glance took everything in: the fabric-covered wings stacked against the walls; the brightly colored fuselages; the 150-horsepower engines waiting to be installed.

Earlier Charles had paid Ray Page, the factory's owner, his entire tuition fee of $500 in advance. The money was part of the sum his parents had set aside for his college education.

Page neglected to tell the naive Charles that he was the only paying student at the so-called flying school. Or that it had just one instructor, a man named Ira Biffle, who also worked in the factory. Or that the sole piece of training equipment was a plane with dual controls.

The main business of the Nebraska Aircraft Corporation was buying up old World War I Army planes and converting them to civilian use. The company produced biplanes, so named because they were equipped with two wings on either side to give the aircraft greater lift. The planes also had two open cockpits, one in back for the pilot and another in front in which two passengers or a small load of cargo could be carried. The engine and propeller were mounted in front. They generated a maximum flight speed of ninety miles an hour.

During his first week at the factory, Charles stitched fabric covers for wings and helped the mechanics tune up engines. His fellow workers liked the tall, lanky young man who was so eager to learn about planes and flying. They gave him a nickname that would stick for years—Slim.

At last, three weeks after his arrival in Lincoln, Charles had a chance to go up in a plane for the first time. He rode as a passenger in the front cockpit with another young man who worked at the factory, Bud Gurney. Belted into the open cockpit, with helmets on their heads and goggles to protect their eyes, Charles and Bud watched a mechanic give the propeller a fierce pull, then jump back as the engine roared into life.

When the engine quieted to a steady hum, other mechanics removed the chocks—blocks of wood that kept the wheels from rolling. The plane lurched forward, bumping over rough ground, moving faster and faster toward a line of trees at the edge of the field. Then the bumping stopped, the ground receded, and the plane rose slowly into the air.

"Trees became bushes; barns, toys; cows turned into rabbits as we climbed," Lindbergh wrote later. "All the country around Lincoln lay like a relief map below."

After that first flight Charles was eager to get more experience in the air, but Ira Biffle proved an unreliable teacher. A tough-talking veteran of World War I, Biffle had seen his best friend die in a plane crash, and after that he seemed to lose interest in flying. He made many appointments with Charles for lessons but kept few of them. As a result, after six weeks in Lincoln Charles had received only eight hours of instruction. And before he could get in any more hours, Ray Page dealt his ambitions a sharp blow.

Page announced that he planned to sell the training plane to Erold Bahl, a flier who was about to embark on a month-long barnstorming tour of southeastern Nebraska. Once the plane was gone, Charles would have nothing to train in.

Ira Biffle spoke up for Charles. He told Page that his pupil had demonstrated an instinctive "feel" for flying and said he thought Charles was ready to solo—take a plane up into the air by himself and bring it safely down again. Page replied that he was sympathetic to Charles also. But he wasn't ready to risk his plane or the young pilot's life on a chancy solo flight.

Charles said he understood. Although he hadn't gotten as much instruction as he'd paid for, he'd learned a lot from working in Page's factory and from the hours he'd spent in the air with Ira Biffle. Now he decided the best way to acquire more experience was to apply for a job as mechanic and general helper on Erold Bahl's barnstorming expedition. Bahl hired him, and the two of them set out in the training plane.

Barnstorming was a way for fliers to make a quick but uncertain living in the early days of aviation. They would go from place to place, flying low over a town and then landing in a nearby field. The fliers hoped the curious inhabitants would come out to see their plane—still a novelty in many rural areas. Then the fliers would try to persuade the more adventurous individuals in the crowd to go up for a short ride. The standard fee was five dollars per person.

Barnstorming brought out Charles's daring streak. He convinced Erold Bahl that they would draw bigger crowds if he, Charles, left the front cockpit and walked out on the lower wing when the plane swooped down over a town. This stunt was known as wingwalking, and was not too dangerous if you held tightly to the wire cables that linked the plane's double wings.

Bahl went along with the idea but warned Charles to make sure he stepped only on the horizontal wooden spars that were the framework of the wing. Otherwise he might go right through the wing's thin fabric covering and damage it beyond repair. Charles followed Bahl's advice, for his own sake as well as the wing's, and they did attract larger crowds from then on.

The tour over, Charles returned to Lincoln, took a job as handyman in Ray Page's factory, and tried to figure out how he could achieve his long-range goal: to pilot his own plane.

Late in June Charles W. Hardin, a maker of parachutes who traveled from place to place demonstrating his products, put on a show of "aer-

Charles refuels the plane while on a barnstorming tour. Another member of the tour, Leon Klink, stands at the right. Minnesota Historical Society.

ial thrills" at the Lincoln Aviation Field. Charles was in the audience, watching excitedly as Hardin performed his famous double parachute jump from the wing of a plane. Starting out with one chute, Hardin cut it loose and switched in midair to another.

"I stood fascinated while he drifted down, swinging with the wind, a part of it," Lindbergh wrote. And although he had never made even a single jump, he determined then and there that he would perform a double jump himself . . . and soon.

A few days later Charles found Hardin at work on a new chute in a corner of Ray Page's factory. When he told Hardin he wanted to start out by making a double jump, the parachute maker was skeptical at first. But Charles persisted. "I want to see what it's like," he said. "I want to learn how to do it."

"All right, Slim," Hardin said at last. "If Page will give you a plane, I'll let you use my chutes."

That evening, with the sun low in the west and the sky clear, one of Ray Page's planes climbed slowly to an altitude of 2,000 feet. Seated in the passenger cockpit, Charles looked first at the small crowd gathered on the field below and then at the big parachute bag lashed to a strut far out on the plane's right wing.

At a signal from the pilot Charles climbed out of the cockpit. Clinging to slender wires as the wind pressed against his body, he made his way carefully out along the wing. When he reached the parachute bag, he hunched down and hooked first one parachute hook and then the other to the harness he wore over his flight suit.

Charles looked back and saw the pilot nod. It was time. He let himself down until he was dangling beneath the wing. Now the only thing holding him to the plane were the two ropes from his harness that ran up into the parachute bag. And the only thing holding the bag together was a single bowknot. The pilot cut the engine and the plane's nose dropped slightly. That was Charles's signal to jump. He forced his hand to reach up and untie the knot on the parachute bag.

White cloth streaked out above him—the first, still-closed parachute. His body tense, he turned in space and lost all sense of time. Then the harness tightened on his legs and waist and he looked up to see a white muslin canopy spreading round and wide. The first parachute had opened.

Swinging gently on the air, Charles looked down at the ground and then at the reddening clouds in the west. But he couldn't relax yet; there was a second jump to make. Reaching up, he cut the line that secured the second parachute to the first, and the first chute drifted away. Once again he was falling freely, without support of any kind. He waited for his harness to tighten the way it had before, but all he felt was air rushing past his body.

Then—jerk! He was pulled upright as the second chute blossomed at last above him. The chief danger was over, but the ground was coming up fast now. Charles braced himself to meet it and let himself fall sideways when his feet touched the earth. He'd been told that was the best way to land. Hardin, Page, and the others who'd been watching came running across the field to greet him. Only after he'd talked to them did Charles realize how close he'd come to having a fatal accident when the second chute was slow to open.

Before the jump, Charles had sometimes dreamed of falling from a high roof or cliff and plunging, terrified, toward the ground. But that night he dropped into a deep sleep as soon as his head hit the pillow, and he never again dreamed of falling.

Charles's life changed in other ways following the jump. Not only did he feel more confident of himself and his abilities, but he sensed that Page, Hardin, and his other colleagues thought better of him, too. He might look young for his age, but he had demonstrated that he could bring off a bold act with calmness and courage. When it came to parachute jumping, he'd left the role of apprentice behind and become an instant expert.

Charles buckles on his parachute before climbing aboard the plane. Photo by John M. Noble, the Minnesota Historical Society.

Later that summer Charles made a proposal to Ray Page and Charles Hardin. He would trade his claim to a solo flight and the wages Page owed him for several weeks' work in the factory, put in twenty-five dollars of his own, and get one of Hardin's well-made parachutes. Charles needed the chute so that he could accept an offer to go barnstorming in Kansas.

Page and Hardin agreed to the deal, and Charles—after storing his motorcycle at the factory, paying his boardinghouse bill, and packing his new parachute and suitcase—set off by slow-moving train to Bird City, Kansas. There he joined a barnstorming outfit financed by a local farmer, Banty Rogers, and piloted by H. J. Lynch, whose skill Charles admired. For his part Charles would serve as mechanic, general helper, and stuntman on the tour. He hoped to learn as much as he could about flying from observing Lynch at work, and save some money toward a plane of his own.

Billed as "Daredevil Lindbergh," Charles thrilled audiences in small towns across western Kansas, eastern Colorado, Wyoming, and Montana with his wingwalking and parachute jumps. He and Lynch had a mascot who accompanied them on their flights—Banty Rogers's fox terrier, Booster. At the sight of the plane, the dog would go wild with excitement. Charles rigged up a special harness for him so that he could ride behind the pilot's cockpit, strapped to the fuselage. Booster kept his eyes peeled on the scene below, and whenever he saw cows grazing or a jackrabbit hopping along, he would erupt in loud barking.

After the tour ended in the fall, Charles went back to Lincoln, reclaimed his motorcycle, and rode home to Minnesota. Not much flying went on in the Middle West during the winter months because of the weather.

Charles spent most of the winter on the farm in Little Falls, making frequent trips to Minneapolis to see his father. He'd heard that surplus Army training planes were on sale cheap at an airfield in Georgia, and he hoped he could persuade C.A. to co-sign a bank loan for $900 so that he could travel down to Georgia and buy one.

C.A., who still hadn't reconciled himself to Charles's pursuing a career in aviation, tried one last time to get his only son to change direction. But he respected Charles's determination, and when the attempt failed, he signed the loan with him.

After visiting his mother for a few days in Detroit, where she had gotten a job teaching chemistry at Cass Technical High School, Charles headed south at the end of April. He had spent only about eight hours at the controls of a plane with Ira Biffle, and a few more with H. J. Lynch during the barnstorming tour. But his limited experience didn't dampen his excitement. He was about to buy his own plane, and he was confident he could fly it.

✧ CHAPTER FOUR ✧

Army Pilot

Souther Field in Americus, Georgia, looked like a ghost city when Charles got there. During World War I thousands of military men had lived in its long rows of wooden barracks, but now only three or four civilian mechanics worked in the field's dozen hangars. Their job was to recondition the surplus training planes the Army was selling off.

Charles had his choice of more than a hundred planes, and after bargaining on the price, he bought a biplane known as a Jenny for just five hundred dollars. The Jenny acquired its nickname from its initials; its official model name was the Curtiss JN–4D. Equipped with a ninety-horsepower engine, the Jenny flew at low altitudes at a top speed of seventy-five miles an hour.

For his five hundred dollars, Charles got not just the Jenny but a brand-new engine and a fresh coat of paint on all the plane's fabric surfaces. After the paint was dry, the chief mechanic turned the plane over to Charles and asked, "When are you going to test her out?"

The mechanic assumed Charles was an experienced flier. If he weren't, why would he buy a plane? Neither the mechanic nor anyone else at Souther Field asked to see Charles's flying license. In 1923 you didn't need a license to pilot an airplane.

Charles hesitated for a moment. He hadn't flown in six months and had never soloed. But he did know the basic theory of flying—and he thought he could get the Jenny up into the air and down again without cracking up. So he told the mechanic, "Let's push her out on the line."

Once the plane was out of the hangar, Charles climbed into the cockpit, warmed up the engine, and taxied to the farthest corner of the field. He planned to taxi back and forth a few times before taking off. That would give him time to get a feel for the plane's controls.

He headed down the field into the wind and opened the throttle. The plane swerved a little, so he straightened it and opened the throttle some more. When the tail lifted up, he pulled back on the stick until the tail lowered, then pushed it forward again. Suddenly the plane was in the air!

Not expecting this, he cut the throttle. The plane dropped too fast, with the right wing low, and bounced down on one wheel and a wing. Nothing was seriously damaged, but it was a hard landing for the frail wooden craft to absorb.

Embarrassed, Charles wished he could just sit there in the middle of the field until he figured out what to do next. But the mechanics would be sure to wonder what was wrong and come out to investigate. He decided it would be better to turn the plane around and taxi back to the hangars. If the mechanics said anything about his aborted solo, he'd tell them he planned to take the Jenny up later.

Fortunately for Charles, another pilot was at Souther Field that day. He'd seen what had happened and realized that the young Lindbergh needed help. The man offered to sit in the front cockpit when Charles took the plane up again.

Charles was reluctant at first; he hated to admit his inexperience to this stranger. But the other pilot jumped into the passenger cockpit and Charles taxied the plane out onto the field. In the next hour and a half he made more than a half dozen takeoffs and landings, with the other pilot offering comments and suggestions when necessary. After the last landing he told Charles he shouldn't have any more trouble.

Early that evening Charles decided to make a few hops by himself. Once more he taxied to the far end of the field, glanced at the instruments to make sure all was in order, and opened the throttle.

After he was airborne, he climbed higher and higher over the red plowed hills and thick green woods of Georgia. He didn't stop until the altimeter showed he had reached 4,500 feet, and he might have pushed the Jenny even higher if the sun hadn't begun to set in the west. It was hard to make a smooth landing in the dim light of dusk.

When he was on the ground again, Charles looked up at the patch of sky he had just left. Thanks to the other pilot's reassurance, he had successfully completed his first solo flight. He knew his landing hadn't been perfect—far from it. But at least he hadn't cracked up.

Charles spent the next week at Souther Field practicing takeoffs and landings, and racked up five more hours of solo flying. Then, with his funds running low, he decided to barnstorm through the South for a while and make a little money before returning home to Minnesota. He spent over a week near the small town of Maben, Mississippi. People flocked in from the surrounding countryside just to see the Jenny fly, and Charles took up close to sixty passengers for short flights. He stopped the Jenny's engine only when it was necessary to pour more gasoline into the fuel tanks.

In early June Charles joined his father in Marshall, Minnesota. The elder Lindbergh was in the midst of a heated primary race for a seat in the United States Senate. C.A.'s manager thought his candidacy would get a much-needed boost if he campaigned by air with his flier son, and Charles was all for the idea.

C.A. had never flown before, but he bravely entered into the spirit of things, tossing leaflets down on the crowd that was waiting at their first stop. His aerial campaign lasted little more than a day, however. Shortly after taking off from a pasture near the town of Glencoe, the Jenny suddenly nose-dived from fifty feet up. It slammed back down to earth, breaking the propeller and shattering a wing.

Charles suspected sabotage. When he examined the damaged plane, he discovered that the rudder-control wires had been sliced partway through so that they would break at the first sharp turn. C.A. was reluctant to believe his political enemies had plotted against him. He thought

Charles, his back to camera, assesses the damage to his Jenny after a crash during his father's 1923 campaign tour. Minnesota Historical Society.

the accident was more likely the result of a prank played by some teenage boys.

Luckily, neither Charles nor C.A. had been seriously injured in the crackup. But by the time the Jenny was repaired, primary day had come and gone and C.A.—who completed his campaign by car—had been defeated by a wide margin.

Charles spent the rest of the 1923 summer season barnstorming across southern Minnesota, northern Iowa, and western Wisconsin. He flew over the Little Falls farm where he had spent so many happy months as a boy, landed on an uncultivated field, and had a good visit with the tenant farmer who was working the place.

In August Charles felt sure enough of his flying skills to invite his mother to come barnstorming with him. Evangeline joined him in Janesville, Minnesota, and was a bit nervous before going up for the first time. Once in the air, though, she thoroughly enjoyed the experience. She and Charles barnstormed together for ten days through central Minnesota, and on several occasions he let his mother take over the controls.

Marvin A. Northrop, an airplane manufacturer who also owned a flying field north of Minneapolis, often saw Lindbergh that summer. He described him as a "tall, sunburned, boyish figure" who walked out to the field in long, swift strides. It was Northrop who pointed the young pilot toward the next stage in his flying career. He told Charles about the Army Air Service Training Schools that had just been established, and urged him to enlist as an Air Service cadet.

"You won't have to keep flying these low-powered crates," Northrop said. "Instead you'll fly modern planes—DeHavillands with 400-horse-power engines."

The idea appealed to Charles. Barnstorming was fun, but there was no future in it. He filled out an application to the Training Schools and got a letter asking him to appear before the Air Service examining board at Chanute Field in Rantoul, Illinois. He passed the entrance examination easily and was ordered to report for duty at Brooks Field in San Antonio, Texas, on March 15, 1924.

Before then Charles sold his Jenny for more than he had paid for it and bought a cheaper Canadian plane in which he barnstormed around Mississippi, Alabama, and Texas. During the tour he had a few minor crackups, and when it was time to leave for San Antonio, he wondered if his battered plane would make it. But he managed to fly the aircraft to Brooks Field despite a missing tire and big rips in the fabric of one wing.

Charles had more than 325 hours of flying time under his belt when he arrived at Brooks, so he was permitted to solo his first day there and handily passed it and his other flight tests. Later he entered eagerly into aerobatics, the flying acrobatics that were part of the Army training course. With the zest that had marked his aviation career from the start, he performed all the prescribed spins, loops, and wingovers.

In April, just three weeks after the start of his training, Charles received an upsetting telegram from the Mayo Clinic in Rochester, Minnesota. For some time his father had been suffering spells of forgetfulness. Now C.A. had been diagnosed as having an inoperable brain tumor.

Charles obtained a brief furlough and went at once to Rochester to

Top: *Brooks Field, San Antonio, in 1924.* Bottom: *Charles fondles a pup mascot on the bombing range at Kelly Field in San Antonio.* Both photos from the Minnesota Historical Society.

see his father. Nothing is known of what he and C.A. said in private to each other, or even if C.A. was fully conscious. But the elder Lindbergh's law partner and friend, Walter Quigley, observed: "I could see that Charles was deeply moved by his father's condition."

A month later, on May 24, 1924, C.A. died. He had asked that his body be cremated and the ashes scattered over his Little Falls property. Eventually Charles was able to fulfill his father's wish, taking his ashes up in a plane and releasing them into the wind above the farm.

Back at Brooks Field he plunged into his studies with fresh determination and did extremely well. And the studies were not easy. Of the 104 young men who began their basic training at the field in March, only 33 remained when the training was completed in September. Charles was not only one of the 33, but he came in second in the group.

The successful cadets moved on to Kelly Field, also located in San Antonio, for advanced training. Eighteen of them, including Charles, received their wings and were commissioned second lieutenants in March 1925. This time Charles was first in the class, achieving a 93 average in such wide-ranging subjects as aerodynamics, navigation, and radio theory. For the first time in his school career he had cared deeply about what he was studying and had wanted to succeed at it. Not only succeed, but come out on top.

Since the United States wasn't at war in 1925, most of the graduates resigned their commissions and went back to civilian life. But they remained members of the Air Service Reserve Corps.

Charles followed this course, leaving San Antonio and heading north to Lambert Field in St. Louis. He'd barnstormed there a couple of years before and hoped he might get a job flying for the Robertson Aircraft Company, which used the field as its base.

He was in luck. The Robertson brothers, Bill, Frank, and Dan, had put in a bid to operate the St. Louis–to–Chicago airmail route that was about to be established. If they got the contract, they wanted Charles to be the chief pilot on the route. The only problem: The Robertsons wouldn't know for some months whether their bid had been accepted.

CHAPTER FIVE

Flying the Mail

While he waited for word on the airmail route, Charles gave flying lessons at Lambert Field and served as an instructor with the Missouri Air National Guard.

In the fall of 1925 he was hired to perform aerial stunts at county fairs in Colorado and Wyoming with an outfit called Mil-Hi Airways and Flying Circus. The job would give him the chance to fly in and around the canyons and peaks of the Rockies and learn how to deal with downdrafts and other forms of air turbulence peculiar to flying in high mountain ranges.

When Charles reported for work in Denver, Captain Wray Vaughn, the owner of Mil-Hi, wasn't impressed. Vaughn described the young Lindbergh as "a tall, gangling kid in a misfit blue suit about three sizes too small for him. On his head he wore a frayed cloth cap, and he carried only a cardboard suitcase and a duffel bag."

But as soon as Vaughn saw Charles put a plane through its paces, he ceased thinking of him as a shy, awkward youth. Billed as "Bud Lindbergh, the Flying Fool," Charles performed all the standard stunts—the loops, spins, and barrel rolls—that he had mastered in the Army Air Service.

He also developed a specialty of his own. After climbing thousands of feet into the air, he dove straight down at such terrific speed that those watching thought he must surely crash. Some screamed in alarm. Then at the last minute he pulled out of the dive, so close to the ground that the wheels on his plane sometimes brushed tall grasses and other plants. "There was never another pilot like him," Wray Vaughn told a reporter later.

Charles returned to St. Louis after the Mil-Hi job ended. He rented a room near Lambert Field in a boardinghouse where other pilots and mechanics lived, and was hired to test planes and give flying lessons for the Robertson brothers.

Charles helps load the first sack of airmail to be flown on the St. Louis–Chicago route, April 1926. Photo by Swenson Studio, the Minnesota Historical Society.

Early in 1926 the Robertsons won their airmail bid and Charles set to work helping them lay out the 285-mile route between St. Louis and Chicago. He set up nine emergency landing fields along the way, one about every thirty miles. These were not really airfields, just level stretches of ground where a pilot could land if he got into trouble.

In April 1926 Charles flew the first airmail from St. Louis to Chicago in a DeHavilland plane like those he had piloted in the Army Air Service. He sat in the open rear cockpit, with the mail sacks stowed in the front cockpit.

The plane took off from St. Louis at four P.M., made scheduled stops in Springfield and Peoria, Illinois, and landed in Chicago at seven P.M., in time to connect with an overnight flight to New York City. If all went according to plan, a letter from St. Louis that was on that flight would reach the New York City post office in time for delivery the next day— one day sooner than a letter carried by train.

The Robertsons' pilots—Charles and two others—made five round-trip flights between St. Louis and Chicago each week. During the summer months they connected with the New York flights 98 percent of the time, earning a reputation for efficiency and reliability.

Between trips Charles relaxed in his room or helped the mechanics tend to the planes at Lambert Field. Unlike most of his fellow pilots, he did not smoke or drink, and he had given up coffee when he was in college. He believed all three stimulants might affect his nerves and slow his reflexes. But he had a huge appetite. At Louie's Place, a diner near Lambert Field, he often dug into a breakfast consisting of a half dozen eggs, toast, a mound of home-fried potatoes, and a pork chop or small steak.

Charles was also fond of playing practical jokes on his airmail colleagues. He spent hours trapping frogs and toads to put in the other pilots' beds. After he discovered that one of the mechanics was deathly afraid of bulls, he borrowed a big, gentle cow from a neighboring farmer and led her up to the plane under which the mechanic was working.

"Hey, look out for the wild bull!" Charles shouted in a loud voice. The white-faced mechanic wriggled out from beneath the plane, took one look at the "bull," and ran for cover while Charles laughed and laughed.

His colleagues never seemed to take offense at Charles's jokes. Perhaps they knew that he hadn't had many pals to fool around with as a boy and was simply making up for lost time.

The airmail operation ran smoothly until mid-October. Then winter weather arrived in the Midwest, bringing snow, sleet, fog, and early darkness, and making it much more dangerous to fly as well as land. Neither the airfields nor the emergency landing fields were lighted. The DeHavilland planes didn't carry landing lights, either.

If a pilot had to bring down his plane at night through low clouds or fog, he dropped a parachute flare and hoped it would light the way. Should it fail to ignite, he was out of luck. Each plane was equipped with just one flare in order to keep down costs.

Lighting wasn't the only problem Charles and the other pilots had to deal with. There were rarely any radio links between their planes and the ground. And they had learned from painful experience not to trust the accuracy of most weather reports they received.

Despite these hazards, the St. Louis–based airmail pilots kept on flying. They all had narrow escapes, and Charles was forced to make several emergency parachute jumps. The most dangerous of these occurred one night in early November when he ran into thick fog south of Chicago.

He tried to drop his single flare so that he could land on one of the farm fields below, but when he pulled the release, nothing happened. He decided to fly on toward Chicago, hoping the fog might be thinner around the airmail field. Instead it was so thick that he could not see any of the lights the Chicago mechanics were trying to beam up to him.

After circling the field for a half hour, he headed west in search of one of the beacon lights on the transcontinental air route. They were all fogged in too. Suddenly his engine coughed a few times, then cut out almost completely. The main fuel tank had run dry.

Reacting quickly, Charles switched to the reserve fuel supply. It would give him twenty more minutes of flying time, but he was pretty sure that wouldn't be enough to get him to the outer limits of the fog. When the reserve tank was empty, he would have to jump.

He climbed for altitude so he'd be farther from the ground when his parachute opened. Just as the plane reached 5,000 feet, he heard the engine sputter out a second time. There wasn't much time now. He unbuckled his safety belt, climbed out of the cockpit, and dove into space.

After two or three seconds of free fall, he yanked the rip cord. The parachute opened almost immediately, and he thought he was out of danger as he drifted down toward the top of the fog bank. Then he heard the sound of an airplane—and realized with a start that it was coming toward him!

A moment later he saw that the plane was his own DeHavilland. He had neglected to turn off the switches before he jumped, thinking the plane was completely out of gasoline. But there must have been a small amount of fuel left in the tank. It drained forward into the carburetor when the plane started to drop, propelling the craft into unmanned flight. Now it was less than a quarter of a mile away, and circling toward Charles.

He grabbed hold of the parachute cords so that he could guide the chute in one direction or another if the plane came too close. Fortunately, he didn't have to; the plane was more than a hundred yards away when it passed him on its downward circle. The game of aerial tag wasn't over, though. The plane spiraled around him five more times before he sank at last into the fog bank.

Knowing the ground was no more than a thousand feet below, he prepared himself for the impact. He held his feet together, protected his face with his hands, and hoped for the best. *Whump!* He landed safely in a cornfield.

After he got to his feet and rolled up his parachute, he set out to discover what had happened to his plane—and its load of mail. A farmer nearby had heard the plane pass overhead but didn't know where it had crashed. He let Charles use his phone to call the operator, and she put

Charles, fourth from left, stands by his airmail plane after its crash near Chicago, October 1926. Minnesota Historical Society.

through emergency calls to the airfields at St. Louis and Chicago, informing them that Charles's plane was down.

A little later the operator called back to tell Charles that the wreckage had been spotted about two miles from where he was. He and the farmer drove at once to the site and inspected the remains. Little was left of the plane, but the mail sacks had been thrown clear and the mail was undamaged. Charles took the sacks to the nearest post office so they could be put on the next train to Chicago.

Happily, most of Charles's flights were not so dramatic. On quiet nights, when the sky was clear and the moon rising in the east, he could even sit back in the cockpit and allow his thoughts to wander. Sometimes he felt he could fly on forever, past Chicago, past Indiana and Ohio, over the Allegheny Mountains, all the way to New York City.

But why stop there? As he looked up at the stars shining brightly in the autumn sky, he imagined himself the pilot of a powerful plane filled with fuel tanks. In it he would leave the North American continent behind and fly all the way across the Atlantic Ocean to—where? To Paris, that's where. To Paris, France.

✧ CHAPTER SIX ✧

Looking for a Plane

If Charles carried out his dream, it wouldn't be the first time someone had flown across the Atlantic. In 1919 two British airmen flew from St. John's, Newfoundland, to Ireland, where they made a forced landing in a peat bog. But that was a distance of only 1,960 miles. No one had yet attempted the 3,600-mile route between New York and Paris.

To encourage such a trip, in 1921 a well-to-do Frenchman, Raymond Orteig, offered a prize of $25,000 to the first aviator who made a non-stop flight between New York and Paris. Orteig believed a new and peaceful world community would naturally evolve once the continents were linked by high-speed aircraft. A successful New York–Paris flight would be an important step toward realizing this goal.

Until 1926, however, there were no airplane engines powerful or reliable enough to make the trip. Then the Wright Aeronautical Corporation and other manufacturers developed engines that could perform for eight thousand hours or more without failure. Now, at last, a New York–Paris flight became feasible.

The first airman to take advantage of the new engines and try for the Orteig Prize was a Frenchman, René Fonck. Well known as a World War I ace, Fonck planned to make the trip in a big, specially designed biplane. It had a luxurious cabin with seats upholstered in red leather, a convertible sofa bed, and heated compartments in which full-course meals of Long Island duckling and roast turkey could be kept warm.

There was room for a crew of four: the pilot, Fonck; a copilot who would also serve as navigator; a radio operator; and a mechanic. Three 425-horsepower engines powered the huge aircraft, and it could carry 2,380 gallons of gasoline in its fuel tanks. All told, Fonck's plane weighed more than 28,000 pounds.

Fonck scheduled his takeoff for early in the morning of September 20, 1926, from Roosevelt Field, Long Island, New York. The crowd that had gathered to see him off cheered as Fonck's plane began to lumber down the unpaved airfield. But their cheers turned to gasps when a wheel broke off and the tail dropped down to the ground. There was now no chance that the plane could reach the speed it needed for takeoff.

But still the plane roared ahead as if Fonck were powerless to stop it. It reached the end of the runway, plunged over the rim of a twenty-foot gully, and disappeared from view. Moments later flames shot into the air, followed by a tall column of black smoke. Fonck and his copilot managed to crawl out of the plane before the fuel tanks exploded, but the radio operator and the mechanic were burned to death.

Out in St. Louis, between airmail trips, Charles read the newspaper accounts of Fonck's doomed flight. He felt sorry for the French pilot and especially for the crew members who had died. But the failure of the Fonck attempt didn't stop him from wanting to compete for the Orteig Prize and make his own flight to Paris.

Lindbergh analyzed Fonck's flight preparations in order to learn from the Frenchman's mistakes. For example, he didn't think a big, heavy, three-engined plane was necessary for a transatlantic flight. A pilot would be better off with a lighter, single-engine aircraft as long as it had room for enough fuel.

The pilot wouldn't need upholstered seats and a bed, either. "If there's upholstery in the cabin, I'll tear it out for the flight," Lindbergh wrote in his journal. "I'll take only the food I need to eat and a few con-centrated rations. I'll carry a rubber boat for emergency, and a little extra water."

He wouldn't install an air-to-ground radio on the plane, or include parachutes in the cargo. The radio systems of the day weren't reliable, especially in bad weather. And a parachute wasn't likely to do him much good if he had to bail out over the icy waters of the northern Atlantic.

Unlike Fonck, he wouldn't take along a four-man crew. In fact, he wouldn't even have a copilot. Lindbergh decided he'd fly alone.

Most pilots in 1926 would probably have been afraid to attempt a nonstop, 3,600-mile flight without at least a copilot for company. But from boyhood on Charles had done things by himself, and he liked being on his own.

His father had been the same way. As Charles made plans for the flight, he remembered a saying C.A. had quoted about the advantages of acting independently: "One boy's a boy, two boys are half a boy, and three boys are no boy at all."

Flying alone would have its practical benefits too. More fuel could be put aboard the plane because of the weight saved on crew members. Their absence would also give Lindbergh one less thing to worry about. The only life he'd be responsible for on the trip would be his own.

Once he'd made the decision to fly alone, Charles focused his attention on the plane he'd like to have for the flight. One came immediately to mind: the Bellanca, a new single-winged monoplane powered by a Wright Whirlwind engine. Its test flights had been a great success.

But the Bellanca would cost at least $10,000 or $15,000. Charles had just a little more than $1,000 in savings; where would he get the rest? There was only one answer: He'd have to find sponsors willing to back the venture.

Before he set out in search of them, Lindbergh went over his qualifications for the flight. At twenty-five he had more than four years of aviation experience behind him and had spent nearly two thousand hours in the air. He had barnstormed over half of the forty-eight states that comprised the United States at the time. He had flown the airmail route through fogs and winter storms. Moreover, he had learned all the basic principles of navigation during his Army training as a flying cadet.

His shy boyishness is apparent in this photo of Charles. Library of Congress.

His shyness sometimes turned people off, though, as did his boyish looks. People meeting him for the first time often thought he was just a gangling teenager. He knew it wouldn't be easy to convince business-men and other wealthy individuals that he, Charles Lindbergh, could bring off such a daring, unprecedented flight. And it wasn't—at first.

He launched his campaign by making an appointment with Earl Thompson, a St. Louis insurance company executive who had taken fly-ing lessons from him. Thompson didn't think a single-engine plane like the Bellanca would be up to the flight. He urged Lindbergh to consider using a trimotor aircraft made by the Fokker Aircraft Company instead.

Although he wasn't in favor of the idea, Charles spoke with a Fokker representative when the man came to St. Louis. The representative told him the company could design and make a trimotor with enough range to reach Paris and deliver it by the following spring. But it would cost $90,000, maybe even $100,000!

Trying to keep his face expressionless, Charles asked what the price would be for a single-engine Fokker plane.

"Mr. Fokker wouldn't consider selling a single-engine plane for a flight over the Atlantic Ocean," the salesman said firmly. The Fokker Company's reputation was at stake, he added. It would be far too great a risk. What if something went wrong with the engine? The pilot would have nothing to fall back on.

Charles decided to look elsewhere. He turned first to Major Albert Lambert, the World War I veteran for whom Lambert Field in St. Louis was named. The major knew and respected Charles, and pledged $1,000 toward the flight. This was the first definite encouragement anyone had given him, but it only reminded Charles of how far he had to go before he'd have the price of a plane.

Next he talked with Major Bill Robertson, founder of the St. Louis–Chicago airmail route. Robertson had no money to invest him-self—the airmail route was running in the red—but he arranged a meeting for Charles with the editor-in-chief of the *St. Louis Post-Dispatch*, the city's leading newspaper.

The meeting proved to be anything but positive. Before Charles had even finished outlining his plans, the editor interrupted him. "The *Post-Dispatch* wouldn't think of taking part in such a hazardous flight," he said. "To fly across the Atlantic Ocean with one pilot and a single-engine plane! We couldn't possibly be associated with such a venture."

At about the same time, Charles read that Commander Richard E. Byrd was planning a transatlantic flight. Earlier in 1926 the commander had made a name for himself when he and his pilot, Floyd Bennett, claimed to be the first people to fly over the North Pole.

Byrd would be formidable competition, Charles thought. And the commander would certainly have no trouble raising the necessary funds for his flight. His presence in the race didn't put a halt to Charles's own plans, however. Instead, he decided to contact the Wright Aeronautical Corporation in New Jersey and tell them he was interested in buying the Bellanca for a New York–to–Paris flight.

First, though, he had to figure out the best way to approach the Wright company. They would probably be impressed if he called long distance—long-distance calls were expensive then, and were used only for important matters. He would ask to speak to an officer of the company, and tell the man he was coming east and wanted to meet with him.

The scheme worked, and Charles got his appointment for a week later. He arranged for another pilot to cover for him on the airmail route, bought a good-quality suit, overcoat, and suitcase, and set out by train for New York.

After all that buildup, the actual meeting with the Wright executives was a disappointment. Like everyone else he had spoken to, they thought a three-engine plane would be better for a flight across the ocean. In any case they couldn't sell him the test model of the Bellanca because it was being considered for production by another manufacturer. They suggested Charles talk to the plane's designer, Giuseppe Bellanca.

Charles and Bellanca liked each other, and the designer thought there was a good chance Charles would be able to buy the test model from the new owners. With that hope in mind, Charles felt optimistic as he boarded a train for the return trip to St. Louis.

His optimism did not last long. In the next few months he heard nothing from Bellanca or the plane's new owners. There was a break-through on another front, though. After listening to Charles outline his plans, Harry Knight, a stockbroker and president of the St. Louis Flying Club, and Harold Bixby, a St. Louis banker, promised complete financial backing for the flight. Now all Charles had to do was find a plane.

No longer counting on the Bellanca, he looked elsewhere. First he approached the Travel Air Company in Wichita, Kansas, which was manufacturing a similar monoplane. They turned him down flat. Next he contacted Ryan Airlines, a small firm located in San Diego, California. They built a monoplane that had proved itself on the airmail route up and down the West Coast.

After his experiences with the other companies, Charles braced him-self for a rejection from Ryan Airlines also. They surprised him by say-ing yes, they could build a single-engine plane capable of flying nonstop between New York and Paris. And they quoted a reasonable price of $6,000 for the plane, exclusive of the engine, which would probably cost another $4,000.

Charles was delighted with Ryan's prompt, favorable reply and even more pleased when the company wired that it could deliver the plane in just two months. He and his backers decided Charles should go out to California and meet the Ryan people face-to-face. He was about to leave for San Diego when word came from New York on February 6, 1927, that the Bellanca might be available after all.

Plans for the flight would go much faster with a plane that was already built. So Charles put the Ryan deal on hold and headed for New York, hopeful that when he returned, he would have his plane at last. But he found a fresh obstacle standing in the way. Charles Levine, chair-man of Columbia Aircraft, the new owner of the Bellanca, wanted $15,000 for the plane. That was considerably more than Charles and his backers had expected to pay.

Back in St. Louis, Charles told Harry Knight and Harold Bixby the price Charles Levine had asked for the Bellanca. He thought they would probably say it was far too high. Instead, Bixby got out his checkbook and wrote Charles a check for $15,000 so that he could return to New York and buy the plane. And Harry Knight said, "What would you think of calling it the *Spirit of St. Louis?*"

That's a good name, Charles thought. He put the check in his pocket and made plans for yet another trip to New York. This time he wouldn't have to come back by train. If all went well, he'd fly home in the Bellanca.

All did not go well. In New York Charles Levine told Charles, "We will sell our plane, but of course we reserve the right to select the crew that flies it."

While Lindbergh stood dumbfounded by the man's desk, Levine continued: "You understand we cannot let just anybody pilot our airplane across the ocean."

Not just anybody. Charles knew that meant him, and he was furious. He hadn't worked so hard to raise funds for the flight and find the right plane only to have someone else sit in the pilot's seat. If Columbia Aircraft demanded the right to select the crew, then he would have to look for another plane.

Levine asked Charles to wait, think it over, and call him again in the morning. Charles agreed, hoping that Columbia Aircraft might change its mind. But when he phoned Levine the next day, the Columbia chairman asked Charles if he had changed *his* mind.

Too angry to reply, Charles slammed down the phone. He'd thought his problems would be solved with the purchase of the Bellanca. Now he had to start all over with the only other firm that had responded in the affirmative: Ryan Airlines out in San Diego.

But it would take the Ryan firm at least two months to build his plane. By then Commander Byrd might be ready to take off in his new trimotor Fokker. There were rumors, too, that Captain René Fonck was preparing for another transatlantic flight attempt. And of course

Charles Levine and the Columbia Aircraft people could hire another pilot to fly the Bellanca to Paris.

In the face of all the competition, Charles wondered if he should change his goal. Instead of going to Paris, maybe he should make plans for a flight across the Pacific. Back in St. Louis he proposed this idea to Harry Knight and Harold Bixby, but they urged him to stick with his original plan. "We're not whipped yet," Bixby said.

Charles was greatly reassured. He hadn't really wanted to give up on the Paris flight, but he wasn't sure if his backers would continue to support it after the Bellanca deal collapsed. Now he realized just how firmly Knight and Bixby stood behind him.

With fresh heart Charles left for San Diego a few days later. There he would judge for himself whether Ryan Airlines was capable of building the *Spirit of St. Louis*.

Cutaway drawing of the Spirit of St. Louis. National Air and Space Museum, Smithsonian Institution.

CHAPTER SEVEN

The Spirit of St. Louis

Charles wasn't impressed by the old, run-down building that housed Ryan Airlines. It was near the San Diego waterfront, and the smell of dead fish mixed with the odor of the varnish used to coat the fabric of airplane wings.

He was impressed, though, with the young men who ran the factory, especially the chief engineer, Donald Hall. When Hall heard that Lindbergh intended to fly alone, he calculated quickly and told Charles that that would allow for at least 50 more gallons of fuel. The two decided the plane should carry 425 gallons in all—enough to cover the 3,600-mile distance between New York and Paris and 400 miles more in case Charles had to make any detours because of bad weather.

After getting a final cost estimate of $10,580 for both plane and engine, Charles gave the Ryan firm an order, and work began immediately on the *Spirit of St. Louis.*

Charles had the final say in every major design decision. It was he, for example, who insisted on putting the cockpit at the back, even though it meant he'd have no forward vision. Sitting in back would be safer, he said, than sandwiched between the engine and the fuel tanks up front. And he'd have no trouble seeing out as long as there were windows on both sides of the closed cockpit.

While Hall worked on the mechanical drawings for the plane,

Charles bought ships' charts and carefully plotted the route he would follow on the flight. It curved northward over New England, Nova Scotia, and Newfoundland, headed eastward across the Atlantic, dropped down past the southern corner of Ireland, went over a small strip of England, crossed the English Channel, and ended inside France on the dot that marked Paris.

In early March Charles read a newspaper article about the latest developments in the transatlantic competition. Commander Byrd's Fokker monoplane was expected to be ready for a May takeoff, the article said, and the Sikorsky Company was building a new three-engine plane for René Fonck.

At the end of the article Charles found his own name mentioned for the first time in connection with the Orteig Prize. "Charles A. Lindbergh, a St. Louis mail pilot, has filed the latest entry, according to the National Aeronautic Association. He will pilot a single-engined Ryan monoplane, and plans to make the flight alone."

But would his plane be ready in time?

Construction of the *Spirit of St. Louis* was moving ahead as fast as Hall could finish the next set of drawings. Everyone at the Ryan factory was putting in long hours of overtime. By mid-March skeletons of both the fuselage and the wings had taken shape on the factory floor.

Meanwhile, Charles read that two more transatlantic flight attempts were in the works. On the American side Lieutenant Commander Noel Davis told reporters he planned to take off for Paris in early June from a Long Island airfield. At virtually the same time a French air ace, Captain Charles Nungesser, announced that he would try for the Orteig Prize by flying a French-built plane from Paris to New York.

This fresh competition only made Charles more determined to finish and test the *Spirit of St. Louis*. In early April the Wright Whirlwind engine for the plane arrived at the Ryan factory. Charles watched intently as the compact nine-cylinder, 23-horsepower engine was carefully removed from its shipping crate. He knew his life during the flight would depend on how this gleaming object performed.

By then word had gotten out about Charles's flight plans, and reporters began to contact him for interviews. He didn't mind giving them at first. Work on the plane was going smoothly, and he thought publicity would be good for the venture.

In the meantime news reports told of the progress being made by Charles's rivals. Noel Davis took up his Keystone Pathfinder biplane on its first test flight and said that the plane handled beautifully. Construction was proceeding rapidly on Commander Byrd's trimotor Fokker, which Byrd had decided to call the *America*. The commander planned a May takeoff.

Both of these expeditions were ahead of Charles's, but the craftsmen at Ryan Airlines were working day and night to catch up. They knew how badly Charles wanted to be in New York with the *Spirit of St. Louis* by the end of April.

Then Charles heard that Charles Levine was about to hire two experienced aviators, Clarence Chamberlin and Bert Acosta, to fly the Bellanca across the Atlantic. In an interview Levine said preparations would be rushed so that the Bellanca would be the first plane to complete a New York–to–Paris flight.

Once again Charles thought it might be a good idea to plan an alternative flight across the Pacific. He bought charts and plotted a course by way of the Hawaiian Islands. But why stop with the Pacific? If all went well, he could fly on around the world. . . .

Word that Commander Byrd's big Fokker monoplane had crashed on its first test flight brought Charles back to reality. Byrd and two members of his three-man crew were injured, and the plane suffered serious damage. Charles was upset. Much as he wanted to be the first to fly to Paris, he didn't wish his competitors bad luck.

Byrd's crash also made Charles wonder how the *Spirit of St. Louis* would perform when he put the plane through its first tests. Would it be everything he hoped for, or would it fall short in some unexpected way?

The *Spirit of St. Louis* was almost finished by the third week in April.

Everyone who had worked on the plane signed his name on the front wing spar before it was covered with fabric. They said they wanted to ride along with Charles for good luck.

All the equipment for the flight had been assembled—Charles's flight suit, water canteens, Army rations, a rubber raft, a repair kit, and red flares in case the plane went down in the ocean and Charles had to signal from the raft. He sampled one of the cans of Army rations. The three dry, brown bars inside looked like chocolate, but they had an awful taste.

A news report dated April 19 said that the French pilot Nungesser planned to take off for New York in early May. Another report announced that the Bellanca would be ready to depart for Paris by the end of April.

Charles made a silent vow not to let these reports worry him. He'd test the *Spirit of St. Louis* as soon as it was finished, then fly the plane to St. Louis. There he and his partners would have to decide what to do next, depending on where the New York–to–Paris competition stood at the time.

The status of that competition changed from day to day. On April 24 part of the landing gear on the Bellanca tore loose and fell off during the plane's takeoff on a test flight. The pilot, Clarence Chamberlin, managed to bring the Bellanca down safely, but the aircraft would need extensive repairs before it could depart for France.

A far worse fate struck Lieutenant Commander Noel Davis on April 26. Davis had just taken off from Langley Field in Virginia on the last of a series of trial flights when he lost control of his plane. Those watching saw a huge splash as the plane crashed into a marsh not far from the field. Both Davis and his copilot were killed instantly.

The news of Davis's death stunned Lindbergh. Why had Davis's plane crashed? he wondered. Had one or more of the engines failed on takeoff? Or was the plane so heavily loaded that it wasn't able to climb?

He couldn't afford to dwell on these troubling questions, because the

Charles leans out one of the windows of the Spirit of St. Louis. National Air and Space Museum, Smithsonian Institution.

Spirit of St. Louis was finally ready for its first test flight. On the morning of April 28, Charles took off in it from the Ryan company's field at Dutch Flats. He was amazed at how quickly the plane accelerated and achieved its top speed of 128 miles per hour.

A Navy Hawk fighter dived down from a higher altitude to inspect the *Spirit of St. Louis*. Feeling confident and a little cocky, Lindbergh engaged it in mock combat, as he had many times with other planes when he was in the Army Air Service. The two aircraft spiraled and zoomed around each other for several minutes before Charles broke off the game and turned the *Spirit of St. Louis* back toward Dutch Flats.

The next morning he was surprised to read a story in a San Diego newspaper headlined "Lindbergh Escapes Crash." It began, "Captain Charles A. Lindbergh, former airmail pilot, narrowly escaped disaster when the plane he is grooming for a transatlantic flight almost collided with a Curtiss Hawk fighter from North Island. . . ."

This was the first time an action of Lindbergh's had been distorted by a reporter for the sake of a better story, and he was annoyed. Weren't reporters supposed to stick to the facts? Perhaps . . . but many newspapers failed to observe that rule, as Charles would soon discover.

The *Spirit of St. Louis* easily passed all the speed tests Charles put it through at Dutch Flats. From there he flew it to another airfield, which had a longer runway, for tests with ever-greater loads of fuel. He had hoped to carry as many as 400 gallons but stopped when the total reached 300, afraid he'd blow a tire landing with more on the rough field. In New York he'd be taking off with 425 gallons on board; he just hoped the field there would be smoother.

By May 8 the *Spirit of St. Louis* was in its hangar at Ryan Airlines, ready for Charles to fly it first to St. Louis, and then on to New York. The only thing holding up his departure was a storm system over the Rocky Mountains, but the weather forecasters predicted it would blow over soon. If they were correct, he might still be the first aviator to take off for Paris.

Then he unfolded the morning newspaper and saw that Captain Charles Nungesser had left Paris at dawn in his biplane. The French pilot was bound, of course, for New York, where he was expected to land the following day. Determined not to let this news depress him, Charles got out his charts of the Pacific Ocean. He spent most of that day studying them and making notes for a possible transpacific flight.

Events took an unexpected turn on May 9. After reports came from Nova Scotia, Maine, and Boston, Massachusetts, that Nungesser's plane had been sighted, all news of the French pilot ceased. His plane never reached New York, and those who claimed to have seen it began to doubt their own eyes. Only one thing was certain: Time had run out as far as Nungesser's fuel supply was concerned. That meant his biplane had been forced down somewhere, either on land or at sea.

Now only three aircraft remained in the transatlantic race: the Bellanca and Commander Byrd's *America*, both of which were undergoing repairs, and the *Spirit of St. Louis*.

Charles visited the San Diego weather bureau on the afternoon of the ninth and got encouraging news. The storm over the Rockies had begun to move eastward. If Charles took off the next day, he could probably expect fair weather all the way to St. Louis. He should even have a tailwind to help speed his plane along.

With that good report in hand, Charles made plans for his departure from San Diego. He scheduled the takeoff for four P.M. California time so that he would have three hours of daylight flying, during which he could turn back or land if any problems developed. Eager to get going, he took off a few minutes ahead of schedule.

All went well until just after sunset, when the engine suddenly began to jerk and sputter. Charles circled while he tried to figure out what was causing the trouble. He was afraid he might have to land in the barren Arizona desert, but first he opened the throttle wide, then pulled it back. To his relief, the jerking ceased and the engine began to run smoothly again.

As dawn approached, he was somewhere over eastern Kansas. Comparing the railroad tracks he saw below with those on his maps, he discovered he was fifty miles south of the course he had plotted. That wasn't too bad considering the problems he'd had with the engine over the desert. But he hoped to stick more closely to his route when he flew across the ocean.

At six twenty A.M. California time (eight twenty A.M. St. Louis time), Charles touched down safely at Lambert Field in St. Louis. He had made the trip from California in just fourteen hours and twenty-five minutes, thereby establishing a new speed record. No one had ever flown that quickly from the Pacific coast before.

The trip also marked two personal milestones for Charles. It was the longest nonstop flight he had undertaken thus far, and the first time he had flown through an entire night. Both were tests he had felt he must pass before embarking on the much longer and more demanding flight from New York to Paris.

Several St. Louis reporters and a bunch of old friends from the air-mail route gathered around Charles as he climbed out of the cockpit. They accompanied him to Louie's Diner, where he ordered one of his usual big breakfasts and asked for the latest news on the competition. There was still no definite word on Nungesser's fate, he was told, and the Bellanca hadn't taken off yet.

When Harold Bixby and Harry Knight arrived at the airfield, Charles discussed the situation with them. Plans had been made for dinners in Charles's honor that night and the next, but he felt he should go right on to New York. Bixby and Knight agreed, and Charles decided to leave for New York first thing the next morning.

✧ CHAPTER EIGHT ✧

Who Will Be First?

The sky was clear when Charles took off at eight thirteen A.M. on May 12, 1927, and remained clear for most of the seven-hour flight to New York. This time he experienced no problems with the engine or any other part of his plane.

As he prepared to land at Long Island's Curtiss Field, a crowd of two to three hundred people was waiting for him down below. They surrounded the *Spirit of St. Louis* before it came to a stop, and Charles saw that those in front were news photographers, their cameras poised for action. He shouted at them to stay back from the still-whirling propeller, but the photographers ignored him. They darted from one side of the plane to the other, vying for pictures of Charles in the cockpit.

The airport manager pushed through the crowd and helped make way for Charles when he climbed down from the plane. Wanting to be cooperative, Charles agreed to pose for pictures standing beside the *Spirit of St. Louis*. But he felt more and more uncomfortable as the photographers milled around him, shoving and cursing each other while they shot him from every possible angle.

At that moment a slender, mustached man came up to Lindbergh. He introduced himself as Dick Blythe, a public relations representative with the Wright Corporation, which had made the engine for the *Spirit of St. Louis*. Blythe told Charles he was there to offer any help he could give.

Acting on Blythe's advice, Charles struck more poses for photographers who had arrived late and answered questions from reporters. But when their questions turned away from his flight plans and became more personal—"Do you carry a rabbit's foot for luck?" "Have you got a sweetheart?" "What's your favorite pie?"—he cut the interview short. What did any of those questions have to do with his goal to be the first to fly nonstop to Paris?

Over supper Lindbergh got the latest news of his rivals in the transatlantic race. Nungesser's plane had not been found, nor had there been any further word of it. Commander Byrd's plane was still undergoing tests. And bad weather over the Atlantic, coupled with uncertainty as to who would fly it, had delayed the Bellanca's departure.

When Charles asked why there had been such a mob of reporters at Curtiss Field, Dick Blythe explained that Charles's record-breaking flight from San Diego to St. Louis had made everyone take him more seriously. From a relatively unknown airmail pilot he had suddenly become a major contender in the New York–to–Paris competition. Whether he liked it or not, Charles could expect constant media attention from now on, Blythe predicted.

The public relations man was right. The blitz of press coverage started the next day with front-page stories about Charles's arrival at Curtiss Field. The account in *The New York Times* began: "A window of the plane opened and the smiling face of a man who seemed little more than a boy appeared. His pink cheeks, dancing eyes, and merry grin seemed to say: 'Hello, folks. Here I am and all ready to go.'"

In the following days engineers made good use of the delay caused by the weather to check every mechanical part of the *Spirit of St. Louis*. They also installed a heater for the carburetor. Charles had decided the engine problem that had developed on the flight from San Diego to St. Louis had been caused by cold air. He wanted to avoid any similar problem over the much colder northern Atlantic.

While the engineers worked inside the hangar, a rope and two policemen held back the crowds that gathered at the airfield each day. They

Crowd surrounds Charles's plane after a test flight at Curtiss Field. Library of Congress.

hoped to catch a glimpse of Lindbergh or, failing that, a distant view of his plane. Prominent in the crowds were many girls and young women who told reporters they "simply adored" Charles, in spite of the fact that he seemed "girl-shy," as one of the young women put it.

Charles worked closely with the engineers and studied the Atlantic weather forecasts carefully. At Dick Blythe's suggestion he had his picture taken with his two rivals in the race, Clarence Chamberlin, who would probably fly the Bellanca, and Commander Byrd. Both men had driven out to Curtiss Field to see the *Spirit of St. Louis* and wish Lindbergh well.

The newspapers came up with various nicknames for Charles. Some, harking back to his barnstorming days, called him the Flying Fool. Others dubbed him Lucky Lindy—a name that was to stick with him for years to come.

His new fame made it impossible for Charles to go off quietly any-

Charles and his mother pose beside the Spirit of St. Louis, *May 1927.* Library of Congress.

where by himself. The moment he stepped out of the hangar, he was surrounded by onlookers and had to be protected by the policemen on duty. At the hotel where he was staying in Garden City, newspaper people filled the lobby at all hours and watched the entrance carefully. Charles couldn't even go for a walk around the block without being followed.

Out in Detroit reporters tracked down Charles's mother. They hounded her at the high school where she taught and waited outside her modest frame home, hoping to get a juicy "inside story" about Charles.

Mrs. Lindbergh flatly refused to discuss her son or his activities. But she decided to travel to New York on the night train to see Charles, talk to him, and bid him good-bye and good luck. She wired Charles that she was coming, and he met her at the Garden City train station on Saturday morning, May 14. They drove immediately to Curtiss Field, where he proudly showed her the *Spirit of St. Louis*.

Afterward they posed for the inevitable photographers, then escaped to have a long lunch by themselves in nearby Hempstead. From there they drove back to the railroad station, where Mrs. Lindbergh planned to catch an afternoon train home. On the platform she and Charles were surrounded once again by reporters and photographers.

"Was your son a good boy?" one reporter asked.

"Just look at him," Mrs. Lindbergh replied.

"You had no trouble raising him?" another reporter asked.

"He raised himself," she said.

"Kiss him, so we can get a good-bye picture!" a photographer shouted.

"No," Mrs. Lindbergh said firmly. "I wouldn't mind if we were used to that," she added with a slight smile, "but we come of an undemonstrative Nordic race."

She gave her son a pat on the back and climbed aboard the railroad car while he was signing an autograph for a child. As the train pulled out, she waved at Charles through the window, and he smiled and nodded in return. And that was that. He refused to answer any more of the reporters' questions and walked quickly to his car.

By Monday, May 16, the *Spirit of St. Louis* was ready to take off. There was no chance of that happening in the immediate future, though. The air route to Paris was still covered with fog and storms. All Charles, Clarence Chamberlin, and Commander Byrd could do was wait as patiently as possible for the weather to clear.

Several different New York newspapers, including the popular mass-circulation tabloids, offered Charles thousands of dollars for the exclusive rights to his story. He decided to sell them to *The New York Times* after an incident involving a couple of photographers from the tabloids.

Charles was coming in for a landing at Curtiss Field after a short test flight in the *Spirit of St. Louis* when the photographers ran in front of his plane to get some closeup shots. To avoid hitting them, Charles swerved the plane abruptly, breaking off the tail skid in the process.

Charles was upset that neither the photographers nor the reporters with them seemed to have any regrets about what had happened. He was even more upset when he read newspaper stories that implied the accident had been his fault. Like the reporters in San Diego, these tabloid journalists obviously thought nothing of distorting the facts. How could they bear to write such stories?

Charles hated inaccuracies of any kind. "Every aviator knows that if mechanics are inaccurate, aircraft crash," he once wrote. "If pilots are inaccurate, they get lost—sometimes killed. In my profession life itself depends on accuracy." That's why he decided to sell the rights to his story to *The New York Times*. He trusted its reporters to tell it truthfully.

On Thursday, May 19, Charles felt depressed after studying the latest weather forecast. A light rain was falling in New York, dense fog blanketed the coasts of Nova Scotia and Newfoundland, and a storm was brewing west of France. It had been a week since he'd landed in New York. Now it looked as if it might be another week before he could take off for Paris.

At least he was ready to go, unlike his two competitors. The newspapers reported that Commander Byrd planned to make several more test flights in his plane, the *America*. And Charles Levine still had not made up his mind about the crew that would fly the Bellanca with Chamberlin.

To distract Lindbergh, Dick Blythe bought tickets to the hit Broadway musical *Rio Rita* for that evening. He and Charles were on their way to the theater when they decided to check the weather one last time. Blythe got out of the car and called the bureau from a public phone. When he came back he could hardly contain his excitement. "The weather over the ocean is clearing!" he announced. "It's a sudden change."

All thoughts of seeing the musical were forgotten. Lindbergh and Blythe turned their car around and headed back immediately to Long Island. If the weather over the route continued to improve, there was a good chance Charles could take off for Paris early the next day.

On the way to the flying field they stopped for a quick dinner and made plans for the night. The mechanics would need to give the *Spirit of St. Louis* a final inspection and the plane's fuel tanks would have to be filled. At the field Charles was surprised to find no indication that either the Byrd or the Bellanca people were getting ready for a possible take-off. He was told that they were both waiting for confirmation that the weather was improving before taking any active steps.

Charles left for his hotel to get whatever sleep he could, but he found the lobby filled with reporters. Rumors had spread of his takeoff plans, and the reporters pelted him with one question after another. It was almost midnight before he reached his room . . . and he would have to get up at two fifteen A.M. to oversee final preparations for the flight. He reassured himself that he could get by without sleep if he had to. After all, he'd done it many times on the airmail run.

By three A.M. Charles was ready to leave for the airfield. He wore Army breeches, knee-length socks, and a tight woolen sweater. Before he climbed into the cockpit, he would put on his flight suit over the other clothes and don a helmet and goggles.

Frank Tichenor, publisher of *Aero Digest* magazine, drove Charles to Curtiss Field. On arrival Charles asked for the latest weather report. It was still raining on Long Island, but he was told the skies were clearing along the coast and over the Atlantic.

"Is anyone else getting ready to start?" Charles wanted to know.

"It doesn't look like it," a mechanic said.

Charles arranged for the *Spirit of St. Louis* to be moved over the slope that separated Curtiss Field from the adjoining Roosevelt Field. The latter had a longer runway, which would be better for his extra-heavy take-off. Once the plane was safely in place, Charles sat out of the rain in Frank Tichenor's car while the last of the plane's fuel tanks was filled to the brim with gasoline.

The *Spirit of St. Louis* would carry 450 gallons of fuel—twenty-five more than originally planned. When Charles climbed into the cockpit, the aircraft's total weight would exceed 5,200 pounds. That was a heavier load than the Wright Whirlwind engine had ever lifted. Charles only hoped the engine would be powerful enough to raise the *Spirit of St. Louis* up off the muddy, unpaved runway and into the air.

Dick Blythe hurried over to the car and handed Charles five sandwiches he had bought for him to eat on the flight: two ham, two roast beef, and one filled with hard-boiled egg.

Frank Tichenor was surprised. "You're only taking five sandwiches?" he said.

"Yes, five," Charles replied. "That's enough. If I get to Paris, I won't need any more. If I don't—well, I won't need any more, either."

It was now seven thirty A.M., and the drizzle was beginning to let up a little. Charles got out of the car, put on his flying suit, and asked two mechanics to check the plane's engine one last time. After being told that it sounded okay, he turned to Dick Blythe and Frank Tichenor and said matter-of-factly, "Well, then, I might as well go."

✦ CHAPTER NINE ✦

Out Over the Atlantic

As he sat in his wicker seat in the cockpit and revved up the engine, Charles could feel the plane's great weight pressing the tires into the wet ground. But there was nothing he could do now to lighten the aircraft. He might need every last gallon of fuel that had been poured into its tanks.

It was time to take off. Suppressing his fears and hesitations, Charles buckled his safety belt, pulled the goggles down over his eyes, turned to the men at the chocks that held back the plane's wheels, and nodded. The men yanked the chocks away, and the wheels began to roll.

As the *Spirit of St. Louis* crept slowly forward, Charles had second thoughts. How could the plane ever gain takeoff speed? he wondered. By now the aircraft was almost halfway down the runway—the last point at which Charles could close the throttle and halt the plane. Instead, he put aside his doubts and pulled the stick back firmly. To his immense relief, the wheels left the ground.

The plane wasn't safely in the air, though. Twice more it bumped back to earth while Charles struggled to keep it in balance. With less than a hundred yards of runway left, the *Spirit of St. Louis* finally attained takeoff speed and left the ground for good. But it cleared the telephone wires at the end of Roosevelt Field with only twenty feet to spare.

Carefully nosing up, Charles looked out one of the windows as the plane climbed faster over a golf course and skirted the trees on a hilltop beyond it. The *Spirit of St. Louis* reached an altitude of 200 feet, then 300. Charles relaxed a little, studied the instrument board in front of him, and banked the plane until it was on the right compass reading for the first segment of the flight.

Only then did he notice that two planes carrying newspaper photographers were following him. They drew in closer, their cameras sticking out of the cockpits as they tried for good shots of the *Spirit of St. Louis.* Charles was annoyed. Once he was in the air, he'd thought he would be free of photographers and reporters—at least for the duration of the flight.

Fortunately the two newspaper planes didn't stay with him for long. As soon as the *Spirit of St. Louis* passed over the shoreline and headed north across Long Island Sound, they turned back toward Roosevelt Field. Now, at last, Charles had the sky to himself.

When he reached the Connecticut shore on the other side of the Sound, he climbed slowly to 500 feet and pushed out the periscope to see what was ahead. Made by one of the factory workers in San Diego, the periscope consisted of two small mirrors set at right angles in a tube that Charles could extend from the left side of the plane. It was a crude device, but at least it helped make up for the fact that the *Spirit of St. Louis* had no front window.

The cloud cover was still very low. If it dropped another hundred feet or was joined by fog, he might have to cut the flight short. But as he continued to look through the periscope, he saw the ground haze clear and the cloud base begin to rise. Encouraged, he flew on.

Although Charles couldn't know it—not having a radio on the plane—people all over the United States had gathered before *their* radios to hear the latest bulletins concerning his flight. It was almost as if he were flying for them, for the entire nation.

Because his overloaded plane was traveling at a low altitude, it was easy to track along the first part of its route. People in Connecticut,

The Spirit of St. Louis *flies over the misty Long Island shore on its way to Paris.*
UPI/Corbis-Bettman.

Rhode Island, and eastern Massachusetts went out on rooftops or climbed trees, hoping to catch a glimpse of the *Spirit of St. Louis* as it flew over their town or farm. By nine fifty-two A.M., just two hours after taking off from Roosevelt Field, Charles crossed Cape Cod, Massachusetts, and headed out over the Atlantic Ocean, leaving the U.S. shoreline behind.

Neither whitecaps nor wind streaks marred the ocean's surface. Charles flew down close to the gently rolling waves to ask for the ocean's approval of his flight. Reassured by its calm, steady expanse, he climbed back up to an altitude of 100 feet and, in smooth air, relaxed his grip.

As he flew on over the ocean toward Nova Scotia, his legs stiffened and he felt a little tired. But he knew he mustn't allow himself to fall into a doze for even a moment. He sipped some water from the quart canteen that hung by his side but didn't eat any of the sandwiches he'd brought along. It would be easier to stay awake on an empty stomach.

At eleven fifty-two A.M., four hours and four hundred miles out of New York, he saw a huge green mass on the horizon ahead. Nova Scotia. He flew higher to get a better perspective and, by checking the land forms he saw below against the lines on his chart, discovered that he was only two degrees off course. Not bad; when he had planned the flight, he had allowed for a five-degree error in navigation.

Continuing on over the forests and lakes of Nova Scotia, he wondered if anyone living in the occasional small settlements below had looked up and seen his plane. And if they had, had they thought to report the sighting? There was no way of telling.

The windows of the plane were open but had come equipped with removable panels that were in a rack behind Charles. He considered inserting the panels now that the air outside the plane was growing colder, then decided against it. Fresh air circulating through the cockpit would help him to stay awake.

The sky clouded over, and through the periscope Charles saw the black mass of a storm system ahead. As the *Spirit of St. Louis* drew closer to it, the plane began to bump up, down, and sideways from the sudden turbulence.

For the first time, Charles wished he'd brought along a parachute. He abandoned his course and flew eastward in order to avoid the more violent storm clouds. Rain squalls beat down on the plane's wings and fuselage; at times the rain fell so heavily that he could barely make out the ground below.

Gradually the squalls became lighter and less frequent, and patches of blue sky appeared between the clouds. The edges of the storm faded away to the north, and the *Spirit of St. Louis* stopped bumping as the air grew calm once more. Charles let out a sigh. His plane had weathered the storm and seemed to be functioning as smoothly as ever. Then he spotted a new danger ahead—a white band of fog along the Nova Scotia coast.

When he got closer, though, he saw that what looked from a distance like a huge fog bank was only a thin strip of mist above the shore. The blue ocean beyond sparkled in the sunlight, and the sky was completely clear. Leaving Nova Scotia behind, Charles flew out over the Atlantic toward his last landfall on the North American continent—Newfoundland.

Past Cape Breton Island the ocean changed from blue to white. Charles flew down to examine it and discovered he was flying over a field of giant ice cakes, all pushing and shoving against one another. He wondered what he would do if the plane's engine suddenly failed and he had to make a forced landing on this ice field. Fortunately the engine was humming along in its usual steady rhythm.

Feeling drowsy, he thought of taking another drink of water but decided against it. He wasn't really thirsty and should save the water for the next day, when he'd probably need it more. Besides, a drink would only increase his need to relieve himself. There was a receptacle for that purpose in a corner of the cockpit, but he didn't want to use it too often.

Late in the afternoon the ice field gave way to a cold, wave-covered sea. Ahead, on the clear horizon, Charles saw the purplish mountains of Newfoundland rising up from the ocean. Dusk was already starting to shadow the land as he flew across the Avalon Peninsula. It was six fifty-two P.M., and in the eleven hours since leaving Long Island he had traveled 1,100 miles—almost a third of the distance from New York to Paris.

Suddenly, after skirting a granite mountain peak, he came upon the little city of St. John's, Newfoundland, built around the edge of a deep harbor. He dove down over the city's docks and wharves and saw men looking up from their late-day chores to gaze at his plane.

Would the men report that they'd seen a silver monoplane fly low over the city on its way to the ocean? And would the news get back to those Charles knew were waiting eagerly for word—his backers in St. Louis who had financed the flight, the workers in San Diego who had built the *Spirit of St. Louis*, and especially his mother in Detroit? He could only hope it would as he flew out over the Atlantic, leaving both daylight and North America behind.

Earlier that day, Evangeline Lindbergh had taught her classes at Cass

Technical High School after telling the principal's office that she was not to be interrupted unless absolutely necessary. She hurried home following her last class to get the latest news of her son's flight, phoned to her by a reporter at the *Detroit Free Press*.

In the evening she reluctantly gave a statement to the reporter. "Tomorrow, Saturday, will be either the happiest day of my whole life, or the saddest," she said. But she believed she would receive word that "my boy has successfully covered the long journey."

On a New York radio station that Friday night, a male trio known as the Bonnie Laddies sang a song they had composed themselves, and it was reprinted in many newspapers the next day. The song's lyrics began:

> *Captain Lindbergh, we're with you,*
> *Won't you, please, come smiling through?*
> *Keep her going, give her the steam,*
> *You'll soon reach the land of your dream.*

Out over the Atlantic Charles looked down on a sea filled with huge, craggy icebergs. Soon fog materialized, thin at first, then thickening until it hid both the ocean and the icebergs. He climbed slowly above the fog, wanting to keep the sky and its stars in view. But the cloud level kept rising, too. Soon he was playing hide-and-seek with the hazy upper clouds and the half dozen or so stars he could still see.

He thought of starting to rely on instruments alone, but he dreaded flying blind. It would be so easy to fall asleep if there were nothing to see through the side windows but a solid gray wall of cloud.

Determined to keep at least a few stars in view, Charles climbed higher and faster. The plane rose more easily now that it was no longer overloaded with fuel. When it reached 7,500 feet, the stars looked brighter and many more of them were visible. But clouds still gathered ominously just a few hundred feet below the plane's wheels.

Charles knew that such a high cloud bank meant a storm area lay in wait ahead. How large an area might it be? he wondered. How turbulent? Whatever conditions he encountered, he decided not to climb higher than 15,000 feet. Above that altitude, the lack of oxygen in the unpressurized cockpit would dull his perceptions and reactions.

At 10,000 feet the air in the cockpit grew noticeably colder. Charles zipped his flying suit all the way up and put on leather gloves. Looking out, he saw that he was flying now between shadowy cloud mountains. The plane shook violently when he was forced to enter one of the tallest clouds and fly blind. Then he heard the sound of something striking the fuselage. Yanking off a glove, he thrust an arm out the window and made an alarming discovery. The air was filled with the frozen pellets of an ice storm.

The instrument panel on the Spirit *of* St. Louis. National Air and Space Museum, Smithsonian Institution.

He had to get back into clear air as quickly as possible; otherwise the plane would ice over. Slowly, carefully, he managed to turn the aircraft around, and ten minutes later he broke out of the deadly cloud. Never had the stars high above looked more beautiful to him.

For a brief moment, still surrounded on every side by towering clouds, he thought of turning back. It would still be possible. But had he come all this way only to abandon his goal now? No. Instead he set the *Spirit of St. Louis* on a more southerly course and wove in and out among the pillars of cloud.

The air in the cockpit felt a little warmer. When he shone his flashlight on the wings, he was happy to see that the coating of ice had begun to melt. Suddenly he noticed that both his compasses were swinging wildly. What could be throwing them off? Having escaped an ice storm, was it possible that he had now entered what pilots called a magnetic storm?

The only thing he could do while waiting for the compasses to steady themselves was steer by the constellations he saw above. At that moment the moon rose, brightening the night sky and cheering Charles. He looked at his watch—ten fifty-two P.M. It was fifteen hours since he'd left New York. He was flying now at a speed of just 86 miles per hour and had 2,100 miles to go before he reached Paris. But he was already halfway to Ireland.

✧ CHAPTER TEN ✧

On to Paris

In the next few hours Charles fought a constant battle against fatigue. He shook his body, stamped his feet against the floor of the cockpit, tensed and relaxed the muscles in his face. He even shouted out the words of a song his father had sung to him when he was little:

All through the Bay of Biscay
That gallant vessel sailed. . . .

But still the longing for rest, for sleep, persisted.

The compasses gradually steadied and the last of the ice fell off the wings. Morning came, lighting up the sky and ocean and giving Charles more to look at. Soon, though, he flew into a white wall of clouds. Diving in an attempt to get under them, he saw the surface of the ocean again. It was studded with huge waves, and from the direction they were breaking, he judged there was a strong tailwind behind his plane. That would help him make up any time he had lost skirting the storm the night before.

His view of the ocean was brief, for up ahead loomed the weather element he dreaded most—thick curtains of fog hanging low over the water. There was nothing he could do but fly straight into the fog. The cockpit darkened, his entire world turned gray, and the feeling of fatigue returned, fiercer than ever.

He willed his eyes to stay open and flew on through the seemingly endless fog. While he was concentrating on the instruments, he became aware that ghostly phantoms had materialized in and around the cockpit. These presences seemed kindly, not threatening. First one and then another leaned over and spoke to Charles in a soft, friendly voice. They offered advice on the flight and gave him important messages—none of which he could remember later.

Listening to the phantoms, Charles began to feel like a phantom himself. He sensed that he was on the borderline of life and wondered if he was experiencing a kind of death. At any other time he would have been alarmed by these visions and perceptions. But on this long, exhausting flight he was so removed from ordinary life that he could accept the presence of the phantoms without surprise or fear.

The fog started to thin, and suddenly the *Spirit of St. Louis* broke through to sunlight and blue sky. An hour or so later, after flying in and out of clouds and sun, Charles saw what he thought was a coastline down below. How could that be? By his own estimate he was at least a thousand miles from land. He dropped down to investigate and was disappointed to discover that the coastline was just a "fog island"—a mirage.

Back in the United States, hundreds of newspapers on that Saturday morning ran a column by the noted humorist Will Rogers. But on this occasion he struck a serious note. "No jokes today," the column began. "A slim, tall, bashful, smiling American boy is somewhere over the middle of the Atlantic Ocean, where no lone human being has ever ventured before. . . ."

At midday on Saturday a fresh wave of fatigue swept over Charles. His eyes closed and stayed shut for four, five, ten seconds before he managed to force them open. He slapped his face once, and then slapped it harder, counting on the stinging sensation to wake his body. But he barely felt either blow.

For the first time he doubted his ability to endure, to stay awake, to complete the flight. What was the alternative, though? Failure—and

The woven wicker pilot's seat in which Charles sat for thirty-three and a half hours on the flight to Paris. National Air and Space Museum, Smithsonian Institution.

death. Yes, death was the alternative. And he wanted to live. He shook his head and body fiercely, flexed his arms and legs, sucked in the muscles of his chest and stomach and then released them.

The exercises did little good; he still felt as if he were about to pass out. Air—that's what he needed. Air. He leaned to one side of the cockpit, held fast to the sill, and thrust his head out the window. The cold rush of the slipstream filled his lungs, reviving him as nothing else had. Gradually full consciousness returned and he became aware of the green ocean below, the brilliant blue sky above. He would live—he would prevail.

He glanced at his watch. In a few minutes it would be seven fifty-two A.M. New York time—exactly twenty-four hours since he'd taken off from Roosevelt Field. But here, so much farther east, the sun had already passed its zenith.

An hour or so later he looked down at the ocean and thought he saw something moving through the water. Another mirage? No—on closer inspection he recognized the sleek, black shape of a dolphin. The sight of the creature made him rejoice. It was the first living thing he'd encountered since leaving Newfoundland.

Not long afterward, flying low over the water, he observed in the distance what he thought was a piece of driftwood. Then it moved, and he saw that it was a bird, a seagull, flying just above the waves. And there was another bird in the sky to the north. How far away from land do seagulls fly? he wondered.

The sun was lower in the sky when several black specks on the water to the southeast caught his eye. Were they what he thought they were? Unbelieving, he squeezed his eyelids together, then looked again. There was no doubt about it—they were definitely small boats, probably fishing boats.

He banked toward the nearest one and dove down until he could clearly see its mast and cabin. But where was the crew? There was no one on deck. Maybe the fishermen had never seen a plane before, and were hiding down below.

Charles flew over to the next boat. No one was on its deck, either, but he saw a man's head poke out of a cabin porthole and stare up at the plane. Charles glided down to within fifty feet of the cabin and shouted in his loudest voice: "Which way is Ireland?"

The man said nothing in reply and his face looked pale—perhaps from fright. Reluctantly, Charles gave up the attempt to make contact, climbed back to a higher altitude, and flew on eastward. At least he had the satisfaction of knowing he wasn't too far from land.

Then he saw it on the northeastern horizon—a coastline with rocky beaches and rolling green mountains behind them. It could only be one place: Ireland. Charles was dumbfounded. He'd left Newfoundland just sixteen hours ago, and had estimated it would take him at least eighteen and a half hours to get from there to Ireland. The tailwind that had sprung up at dawn must have been much stronger than he realized.

Below him now stretched a long, tapering bay. He compared the shape of the bay with his charts and confirmed what he had already guessed. It was Dingle Bay on the southwestern coast of Ireland, with the island of Valentia at its mouth and a village on the island. He dropped down low over the little community. Its inhabitants—unlike the sailors on the fishing boats—ran out into the streets, looked up at the *Spirit of St. Louis*, and waved.

As he gazed down on the scene, Charles felt connected with life again. "This is earth," he thought, "the earth where I've lived and now will live once more." He circled the village one last time, then resumed his course. From Ireland it was only six hundred miles to Paris. If he didn't run into bad weather, he should arrive at the French capital in just six more hours.

Glancing around the cockpit, Charles realized he hadn't been aware of the phantoms since he'd sighted the fishing boats. He double-checked his charts and was pleased to see he was only three miles off the route he'd laid out back in San Diego. Now he was over St. George's Channel, between Ireland and England. He'd feared the English coast might be obscured by fog, but off to one side he soon saw the cliffs of Cornwall, rising straight up from the sea.

It was late afternoon when he flew over the southernmost corner of England. As he looked down on the neat fields separated by stone fences, he thought of his English ancestors on his mother's side. They might have lived on farms like these. To his left he saw the city of Plymouth and its harbor, from which the *Mayflower* had sailed. It had taken its Pilgrim passengers weeks to cross the same Atlantic Ocean that he had crossed in a single day.

In a few minutes he left the English shoreline behind and was flying over the English Channel. From there it was less than an hour to France. The sun was low in the western sky when he approached a strip of land—a cape jutting out from the French coast. Behind it lay the port city of Cherbourg. Now there was no chance that he wouldn't land on French soil, even if for some reason he failed to reach Paris.

For the first time he thought of the steps he'd need to take when he landed. He worried that he didn't have a visa to travel in France—and

A huge crowd awaits Charles's arrival at Le Bourget Airport in Paris. Missouri Historical Society, St. Louis.

he didn't speak a word of French, either. Nor did he have any French money. But he'd deal with those problems later. The important thing now was to fly on to Paris and get the *Spirit of St. Louis* safely on the ground.

At the start of his thirty-third hour in the air Charles was almost 3,500 miles from New York and had broken the world's distance record for a nonstop flight. In just an hour he should be over the outskirts of Paris. Feeling relaxed, he finally unwrapped and bit into one of the sandwiches he'd brought with him. But because he had not eaten for so long, the ham seemed tough and the bread dry, and he had to wash down each bite with a mouthful of water.

The last light left the late evening sky as he approached the Seine River. He was flying at 4,000 feet beneath a starlit sky when, through the periscope, he saw the glow of Paris on the horizon ahead. Dropping down to a lower altitude, he passed over long, brightly lit boulevards as he flew toward the heart of the great city. He circled one of its most famous landmarks, the Eiffel Tower, then turned the *Spirit of St. Louis* northeastward in the direction of Le Bourget, the airport serving Paris.

He wasn't sure he'd found the field at first, because only one corner was lit by floodlights. But he shouldn't have been surprised. After all, he was at least three hours ahead of schedule. Flying lower, he made out the shapes of huge hangars, confirming that this really was Le Bourget.

He dropped down lower still and decided to try for a landing even though most of the field remained dark. Nervously he alternated between looking out with the periscope and concentrating on the instruments; he had never landed the *Spirit of St. Louis* at night before. Down, down the plane came, and then the wheels touched the ground, more gently than he had expected. Not a bad landing, he thought. It was just ten twenty-two P.M., Paris time.

He came to a halt in a pitch-black part of the airfield and swung the plane around, intending to taxi back toward the hangars. But he didn't get very far. The entire field in front of him was covered with people, and they were all running toward the *Spirit of St. Louis*.

✧ CHAPTER ELEVEN ✧

A Hero's Welcome

66 indbergh! Lindbergh! Lindbergh!"

His name came at Charles from all sides as the huge crowd surrounded his plane. Within seconds smiling, shouting faces blocked the view from the windows. Charles could feel the *Spirit of St. Louis* shake from the pressure of the crowd, and then he heard the sound of ripping fabric. Souvenir hunters had begun to tear off pieces of the plane's covering.

Something had to be done to protect the plane before it suffered serious damage. "Does anyone here speak English?" Charles called through a window.

If there was a reply, he failed to hear it above the general noise. He decided to climb down from the cockpit, find someone who spoke English, and organize a guard around the plane. But before he even reached the ground, dozens of hands reached out for him and he felt himself being hoisted above the crowd.

The men carrying him started to move through the mob, and he lost sight of the *Spirit of St. Louis*. Then someone yanked the helmet from his head, the main body of the crowd surged forward, and Charles found himself standing on the ground at last. He had been rescued by two French aviators. They led him quickly away from the mob and drove him to one of the big hangars at the edge of the field.

There Charles found out why so many people had gathered at Le Bourget Airport. Through the afternoon and evening, the *Spirit of St. Louis* had been sighted over Ireland, then England, then the coast of France. With each new sighting more and more Parisians got into their cars and headed for Le Bourget to greet Lindbergh when he landed.

Safe now in the hangar, he was asked if he wanted something to eat, to drink. Did he need to see a doctor? Would he like to lie down and rest for a while? No, Charles said, but he would like to drive back out on the field and make sure the *Spirit of St. Louis* was safe. Unfortunately that wouldn't be possible because of the crowd, his French hosts replied, but they assured him that mechanics were taking good care of the plane.

Remembering his French rival in the transatlantic race, Charles asked if there had been any further word of Nungesser. No, the French aviators said sadly. Nothing.

The U.S. ambassador to France, Myron T. Herrick, had planned to welcome Charles when he landed, but he got caught in the traffic jam on his way to the airport. Then a young American wearing Charles's helmet was brought to the pavilion where the ambassador was waiting—but the man kept insisting that he wasn't Lindbergh.

It turned out that someone had clapped Charles's helmet on the young man's head. The crowd, thinking he was Lindbergh, had lifted him up onto their shoulders, and the real Charles had managed to escape to the hangar during the confusion that followed. All this the ambassador explained to Charles when the two of them finally met in the airfield commandant's office. Charles had been driven there, unnoticed, from the hangar.

Ambassador Herrick invited Charles to come back with him to the embassy. Charles gladly accepted but asked to be taken to see the *Spirit of St. Louis* first. He was dismayed to find that entire strips of fabric had been torn from the fusclage and his logbook of the flight had been stolen. But after a careful inspection Charles was reassured that no irreparable harm had been done to the plane that had brought him safely to Paris.

Driven by the French pilots who had rescued him from the crowd, Charles arrived at the American embassy before the ambassador. The embassy staff put together a supper for him—his first meal since leaving New York—and then, at the ambassador's suggestion, he spent a few minutes answering questions from the reporters who had gathered in the embassy courtyard. When asked if he felt exhausted, Charles said no, not at all. "I could have flown half the distance again," he added. "You know, flying a good airplane doesn't require nearly as much attention as driving a car."

After the press conference Charles went immediately to bed. It was four fifteen A.M. Paris time, forty-six hours since he had last stretched out to rest. He slept until midafternoon the next day and woke feeling a little stiff but refreshed. Still in pajamas, he dug into a big, American-style breakfast of oatmeal, eggs, bacon, toast, and grapefruit. Afterward he talked with his mother via transatlantic telephone. Then he put on borrowed clothes that didn't fit and went out on the embassy balcony with Ambassador Herrick to greet the cheering crowd in the street below.

As he walked out onto that balcony, Charles entered a world of hero worship and fame unlike anything he had experienced before. Overnight his record-breaking flight had made Charles Lindbergh—"Lucky Lindy," "The Lone Eagle"—the center of not just France's but the world's attention. *The New York Times* devoted all of the first six pages in its Sunday edition to the story. Other U.S. newspapers gave Lindbergh's accomplishment tremendous amounts of space, using up 25,000 more tons of newsprint than usual.

Millions of Americans in churches across the country said prayers of thanksgiving for Charles that Sunday morning, and many ministers made his triumph the theme of their sermons. "No greater deed of personal prowess and adventure appears on the pages of man's conquest of nature than this lonely and heroic flight," said Dean Howard Chandler Robbins of the Cathedral of St. John the Divine in New York City.

Charles stayed on in Paris for more than a week, receiving honors

Charles and Ambassador Myron T. Herrick stand on the balcony of the U.S. embassy in Paris to greet the throng assembled in the street below. Corbis-Bettman.

Top: *Charles is warmly welcomed in Brussels, Belgium.* Bottom: *Londoners stand atop their automobiles to watch Charles's landing at Croydon Airport.* Both photos from Corbis-Bettman.

from the minister of war, the foreign minister, and the president of France, and meeting with some of the leading French aviators. Meanwhile, back home in America, Dick Blythe and his associates were flooded with all sorts of commercial offers intended to capitalize on Charles's newfound fame.

A record company offered $300,000 for the rights to the story of the flight, spoken in Lindbergh's own voice. Looking to the future, and assuming that Lindbergh would one day fall in love and get married, a movie company approached Blythe with an unusual offer. The company would pay Charles a million dollars if he would allow it to film the various stages of the romance, climaxing with closeups of the marriage ceremony.

Within a week after the flight, Charles had received a total of more than $5 million in commercial offers. This was at a time when most middle-class American families lived quite comfortably on incomes of $5,000 or $6,000 a year.

To all the offers Dick Blythe and Charles's other representatives said no. Neither they nor he wanted to do anything that would tarnish his reputation as a clean-cut, idealistic young American hero. But Charles did endorse a number of products he felt had contributed to the success of the flight, including the tires on his plane's wheels and the fuel he had used.

From Paris Charles flew the repaired *Spirit of St. Louis* to Brussels, Belgium, at the urging of the U.S. State Department. He was given another tremendous welcome and was formally received by the king and queen of Belgium. His next stop was London, England, where he was greeted on arrival by a crowd of more than 150,000. At Buckingham Palace he was received by the king and queen. He also met the duke and duchess of York and shook hands with their baby daughter—later Queen Elizabeth II.

The king was especially curious about one aspect of life aboard the *Spirit of St. Louis*. Taking Charles aside, he whispered, "Tell me, how do you pee?"

In London, as in Paris and Brussels, Charles impressed everyone who met and heard him with his modest yet confident manner. He said little in his public speeches, but what he did say was intelligent and to the point. Reporters found him more than willing to answer their questions about the flight and share his thoughts on the future of aviation. But he hadn't changed when it came to questions of a more personal nature. Those he fended off or simply refused to answer.

During his London visit Charles confided in the U.S. ambassador that he wanted to fly home to America via an eastward route, with stops in Europe, the Soviet Union, Alaska, and Canada. Thus he would complete the circuit of the globe that he had begun, and score yet another aviation first.

The ambassador dashed these hopes when he told Charles that President Calvin Coolidge expected him to sail home at once to America on the cruiser *Memphis* so that he could be given a hero's welcome in Washington. The wings would be removed from the *Spirit of St. Louis*, and they and the plane's fuselage would travel back with Charles in the cruiser's hold.

Charles hated to see his beloved plane return to the United States "in a coffin," as he put it. But a request from the president could not be ignored or dismissed, so Charles reluctantly agreed to the plan. On June 4, 1927, with the *Spirit of St. Louis* packed away belowdecks, he set sail from the port of Cherbourg aboard the *Memphis*.

On the same day the cruiser left Cherbourg, Clarence Chamberlin finally took off from Roosevelt Field in the Bellanca plane that Charles had once wanted to fly to Paris. Chamberlin landed the next day in Eilsleben, Germany, beating Charles's nonstop flying record by almost three hundred miles. A little over three weeks later, on June 29–30, Charles's other former rival, Commander Richard E. Byrd, piloted his trimotor Fokker plane across the Atlantic.

Neither Byrd nor Chamberlin took the spotlight away from Charles, however. They flew with companions and copilots, whereas he had made the trip alone. Moreover, both of them failed to achieve their announced goals. Chamberlin was aiming for the German capital, Berlin, but engine trouble forced him to land in a marsh a hundred miles west of the city. Byrd's destination was Paris until he ran into foul weather over the English Channel. He and his two copilots barely managed to bring down the damaged Fokker in shallow waters off the French coast.

Their mishaps only made Lindbergh's performance seem more impressive as he sailed home to America, and to a series of tremendous welcomes.

✧ CHAPTER TWELVE ✧

One Cheering Crowd After Another

Charles returned in triumph to America on Saturday morning, June 11. When the *Memphis* sailed up the Potomac River to Washington, church bells rang, fire sirens screamed, and dozens of military pursuit planes and bombers circled the skies overhead.

Scores of small boats sailed close to the *Memphis* so that their passengers could get a glimpse of Charles, standing on the cruiser's bridge. He was easily identifiable amid the uniformed naval officers because he was wearing a well-tailored civilian suit. He could have worn the uniform of a colonel in the Officers' Reserve Corps, a rank to which he had just been promoted. But he had made his flight as a civilian, not as a soldier, and his advisers convinced him to appear in civilian clothing. They said that would make him look more like "everybody's hero."

As the *Memphis* approached the Navy Yard dock, cannons boomed a twenty-one-gun salute to Charles, the first time this honor had been bestowed on anyone but a president or a visiting head of state. Evangeline Lindbergh, who had arrived in Washington from Detroit the day before, was escorted aboard the vessel for a brief, private reunion with her son. Then the two of them walked down the gangplank and got into an open car for a parade up Pennsylvania Avenue.

Charles grinned and waved occasionally to the throngs on either side as the parade turned toward the Mall and ended at the Washington Monument, where a speaker's platform had been erected. When Charles saw the huge crowd that surrounded the Monument—the largest that had gathered in Washington up to that time—he was heard to say, "I wonder if I deserve all this."

President Calvin Coolidge was the main speaker at the ceremony. He paid tribute to Charles in a long speech that was heard by more than 30 million people throughout the United States over a special fifty-station radio hookup. Coolidge called Charles "a boy representing the best traditions of the country . . . a valiant character, driven by an unconquerable will and inspired by the imagination and spirit of his Viking ancestors."

Thousands gather on Washington's Mall to see and hear Charles, June 11, 1927. Library of Congress.

Charles looks out on a sea of people as he delivers his brief speech in Washington. Library of Congress.

At the end of his talk the president turned to Charles, the pilot arose, and the president pinned the Distinguished Flying Cross on his lapel. It was the first time this award had been given.

In response Charles gave a brief speech of just 106 words. He told of his warm reception on the continent and in England, conveyed the best wishes of the people of Europe of the people of America, and closed by saying simply, "I thank you."

The crowd was caught off guard when the speech ended so quickly, and did not react immediately. Then they broke into loud applause. Carried away by the excitement of the occasion, newspaper and radio reporters compared the talk to Lincoln's Gettysburg Address. They called Charles's words simple, touching, and even eloquent.

President Calvin Coolidge and his wife, Grace, entertain Charles and his mother at lunch after the Washington welcoming ceremony. Charles is wearing the distinguished Flying Cross that the president has just presented to him. Photo by Underwood and Underwood, the Missouri Historical Society, St. Louis.

After the ceremony President and Mrs. Coolidge entertained Charles and his mother at lunch. Also present was Dwight Morrow, a prominent Wall Street banker who was about to be named U.S. ambassador to Mexico—and whose family would play an important role in Charles's future.

From Washington Charles flew to New York City, where he received another tumultuous welcome. It was estimated that between 4 and 5 million people were crammed together in the crowd that lined his parade route up Broadway. He smiled and waved to the cheering throng from the backseat of an open car while tons of ticker tape and confetti showered down on him from the windows of tall office buildings.

The next four days in New York were filled with one reception after another. At an affair held at the Brevoort Hotel, Raymond Orteig himself presented Charles with a check for $25,000—the Orteig Prize that had been part of the inspiration for his flight to Paris.

The City of New York gave a grand banquet in Charles's honor attended by 4,000 prominent New Yorkers. Charles Evans Hughes, a well-known lawyer and statesman (and future chief justice of the U.S. Supreme Court), was the chief speaker at the banquet. "We measure heroes as we do ships, by their displacement," Hughes said. "For the time being, Colonel Lindbergh has lifted us into the freer and upper air that is his home. He has displaced everything that is petty, that is sordid, that is vulgar. . . . Where are the stories of crime, of divorce? For the moment we have forgotten them. . . ."

Hughes's remarks helped to explain why Charles Lindbergh literally overnight had become a hero to so many millions of people. The 1920s, like the 1990s, was a decade of rapid social and technological change. Many men and women in the 1920s looked back to what seemed a simpler, more honest time when the media focused on individuals who had done something good and noble—not gamblers who had made a million dollars playing poker or heiresses starting on their fifth husbands.

Charles Lindbergh was exactly the sort of hero these people had dreamed of finding. He was young, handsome, and pure—a pilot who

Top: *Charles rides in an open car up Broadway in New York City as pieces of ticker tape rain down from skyscraper windows.* Bottom: *The check for $25,000 that Charles received from Raymond Orteig.* Both photos from the National Air and Space Museum, Smithsonian Institution.

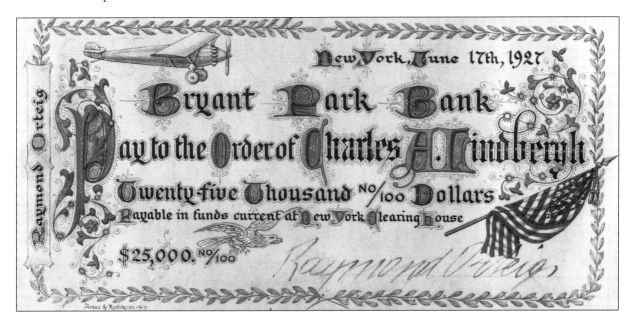

neither smoked nor drank, and whose "best girl" was his mother. And he had accomplished something no human being had ever accomplished before. No wonder they responded to him so strongly, cheering him wherever he went.

A cartoon from the humor magazine Life *comments on the fact that Charles and his heroic flight had shoved all other topics out of the news spotlight. Library of Congress.*

"Blah, they'll soon forget him! He's only a hero!"

On June 16 Charles left New York and flew his plane back to St. Louis—the city for which it was named, and the city whose business-men had raised the funds for his flight. There he was given yet another grand reception. From St. Louis Charles went to Dayton, Ohio, to pay his respects to the surviving inventor of the airplane, Orville Wright, and to spend the night as his guest.

After the St. Louis and Dayton visits, Charles went into seclusion at La Falaise, the Long Island estate of Harry Guggenheim, one of the heirs to a vast fortune and president of the Guggenheim Fund for the Promotion of Aeronautics. Lindbergh had signed a contract for a book about his Paris flight but was unhappy with the first draft of the manuscript, ghostwritten by a *New York Times* reporter. He decided to start over and rewrite the entire book himself.

Working ten to fourteen hours a day in the peace and quiet of the Guggenheim estate, Charles completed the 60,000-word manuscript in a little more than three weeks. It was titled *We*, which expressed the close bond Lindbergh felt between himself and his plane. Rushed into print by the end of July, *We* was one of the first examples of an "instant book" and sold more than 190,000 copies in less than eight weeks.

When he was through with the book, Charles took off in the *Spirit of St. Louis* on a nationwide air tour sponsored jointly by the Guggenheim Fund and the U.S. Department of Commerce. The tour's purpose was to stimulate interest in aviation and demonstrate the safety and punctu-ality of professional flying. Charles was a perfect example of the latter. By the time the tour ended, he had flown 22,350 miles in 260 flying hours. He had made scheduled stops in eighty-two cities and had been late only once, when dense fog delayed his arrival in Portland, Maine.

During the tour an estimated 30 million people saw Charles and the *Spirit of St. Louis*. In his speeches he didn't dwell on his Paris flight but looked ahead to the development of commercial aviation in the United States. "What we need now more than any other thing," he often said, "is a series of airports in every city and town in America."

If Charles was a hero before the tour, he had become a superhero by the time it was over. Novelty manufacturers produced millions of Lindbergh flags, buttons, dolls, and other items to cash in on the American public's love for Charles. A secretary who helped answer his mail told the Associated Press that he had received at least three and a half million letters since the Paris flight. Those from women outnumbered those from men four to one, and among them were dozens of proposals of marriage, many accompanied by snapshots.

More than four thousand poems about Charles and his plane were submitted for cash prizes in a national competition. One hundred of the best entries were published in the fall of 1927 in an anthology titled, not surprisingly, *The Spirit of St. Louis.* A poetic toast by one Edna Stimson suggests the tone of the collection:

> *To you, embodiment of all*
> *We've prayed America might be,*
> *Clean, courage-bred, sincere,*
> *Possessed of praise-proof modesty. . . .*

But Lindbergh was not really as modest and selfless as that poem portrayed him. While he turned down most of the commercial offers that he received after the flight, he earned a considerable amount of money from the Orteig Prize, newspaper articles he co-authored, his book *We,* and the payments he got for making goodwill flights such as the national tour. By the beginning of 1928, it is estimated, his personal wealth had grown from the $2,000 he had in the bank before the flight to over $400,000.

Fame changed Charles's outlook in other important ways. As a boy he had shared his mother's unpretentious, middle-class life in Washington and Little Falls. As a young man he had led the footloose existence of a barnstormer, army cadet, and airmail pilot. Now, after the flight, he had suddenly entered the realm of the rich and powerful. Not only had he been entertained by the king and queen of England and the president of the United States, but he had been invited into the homes of wealthy men such as Harry Guggenheim.

Two young American tourists pose at the railing of an ocean liner with the Lindbergh doll they've brought back from Paris. Library of Congress.

Another such invitation came to Charles in the late fall of 1927. Dwight Morrow, now the U.S. ambassador to Mexico, asked him to make a special visit to that country. Relations between the United States and Mexico were strained at the moment, and Morrow thought a visit by Lindbergh would help to improve them.

The idea of the trip appealed to Charles. He had long wanted to fly in the tropics, and the trip would give him the chance to make another nonstop night flight in the *Spirit of St. Louis*. He wired his acceptance to Ambassador Morrow, little knowing that the journey would also introduce him to his future wife.

CHAPTER THIRTEEN

Anne Morrow

Ambassador Morrow was waiting to greet Charles when the *Spirit of St. Louis* landed in Mexico City on December 14 after a twenty-seven-hour flight from Washington. So were Morrow's wife, Betty; their fourteen-year-old daughter, Constance; and more than 150,000 cheering Mexicans, some of whom had been at the airport since dawn.

This was only the beginning of a six-day welcome marked by speeches and official receptions. Auto manufacturer Henry Ford lent Lindbergh's mother a plane and a pilot so that she could fly down from Detroit to join her son and spend the Christmas holiday with the Morrows. Also present for the festivities were the Morrows' son, Dwight Jr., and their other two daughters: vivacious Elisabeth, who was the oldest, and shy, petite Anne, a senior at Smith College.

With the Paris flight behind him and a career promoting aviation under way, Lindbergh had begun to think of marriage. He was twenty-five, after all, and looked forward to finding "the right girl" and starting a family. Both of the older Morrow daughters seemed likely prospects, and guests at the ambassador's holiday parties thought that Lindbergh was drawn to Elisabeth. A good conversationalist, she had managed to get the usually silent Charles to chat freely.

Among those who noted the attraction was Anne, and she confessed

Anne Morrow. Corbis-Bettman.

in her diary to feeling a little envious of her beautiful older sister. For Anne, like Lindbergh, had trouble making small talk. A bookish sort who wanted to be a writer, Anne hadn't expected to like Lindbergh, the man of action. She was immediately impressed by his quiet assurance, though. And when he offered to take the Morrows up for a ride in the big trimotor plane that had brought his mother to Mexico, Anne claimed a seat up front where she could watch him at the controls.

By the time the flight was over, Anne had become fascinated with flying. It had been a complete and intense experience, she wrote, and she wouldn't be happy until it happened again. Perhaps she had become equally, if not more, fascinated with the man she called Colonel Lindbergh. But being a proper young woman of her time, she did not say so in her diary.

Following his Christmas stay with the Morrows, Charles embarked on a goodwill tour of Latin America in the *Spirit of St. Louis*. During the next six weeks he flew to fourteen Central and South American countries and the Canal Zone, receiving a tremendous welcome at each stop.

The tour ended in St. Louis in February 1928, and Lindbergh's plane went on public display for two months in the city where he had gotten the idea to build it. Then, on April 30, Charles made his last flight in the *Spirit of St. Louis*. He piloted it nonstop to Washington, D.C., where he presented his beloved plane to the Smithsonian Institution. It was almost exactly eleven months since his historic flight to France.

American aviation was changing rapidly in that spring of 1928. The barnstorming pilots who had pioneered the field up to now were losing control to the bankers, promoters, and politicians who had the resources to develop aviation into another big business.

Charles saw this change coming and joined forces with it. In June he accepted a well-paying assignment with Transcontinental Air Transport, Inc. (TAT), a new company that would later become Trans-World Airlines. As chairman of the company's technical committee, Charles was responsible for laying out new air routes, choosing planes to be purchased, and setting safety standards.

Most of his work for TAT involved air routes within the United

States. Later in the year he took on a second job, this one with Pan American Airlines. He would help Pan American develop its growing network of international airmail routes, especially in Central and South America. Talking about the Pan American job with reporters, Lindbergh said, "The thing that interests me now is breaking up the prejudices between nations, linking them up through aviation."

As Charles settled into his new duties, he thought again of marriage and found himself remembering Anne and Elisabeth Morrow. Anne was blue eyed, dark haired, extremely pretty, he wrote in his autobiography, but she seemed to stand in the shadow of her outgoing older sister, Elisabeth.

Still, it was Anne he thought of more and more frequently. At length he decided to act on his feelings, and in the fall of 1928 he laid plans to meet her again. One day in October he phoned the Morrow home in Englewood, New Jersey, and asked to speak to "Miss Morrow."

When the butler informed Anne of the call, she was momentarily confused. She had often thought of Charles in the months since their Christmas meeting—months during which she had graduated with honors from Smith—but she assumed he was more interested in her sister Elisabeth. Now she was sure the "Miss Morrow" he wanted was Elisabeth, not her. But Elisabeth was away, traveling in Europe.

When she finally picked up the phone, Anne discovered to her delight that she was wrong. Charles was calling to invite her, Anne, to go for a ride in his plane. "I—I'd love to," she said.

They met for lunch at Harry Guggenhcim's Long Island estate. Anne was impressed by the elegant surroundings, with peacocks parading on the lawn outside.

After lunch they took off in a borrowed biplane from a field in back of the Guggcnheim mansion. That way, Charles explained, they could avoid any reporters who might be watching for him at one of the local airfields. They climbed until they could see both shorelines of Long Island, and Charles showed Anne how the plane's controls worked. He even let her steer for a while.

Their relationship moved forward rapidly after that flight. A few days later Charles met Anne in Englewood and took her for an evening drive over some little-traveled New Jersey back roads. Before the drive was over, he had proposed to her—and she had accepted. But they decided to keep their engagement a secret, even from Anne's parents, until they could inform them together.

Anne was planning to leave for Mexico in November, and Charles found an excuse to join her there soon afterward. They met with her parents at the Morrows' weekend house in the town of Cuernavaca. Anne's father was at first startled, then pleased by the couple's news. He liked the idea of having a national hero for a son-in-law. Her mother had reservations, however. She wondered how Charles—who had never finished college, and knew almost nothing about books, music, and art—could communicate with Anne on an intellectual level.

If Betty Morrow thought her hesitations would get Anne to change her mind about Charles, she was mistaken. They only made Anne more determined than ever to marry him. Not that she didn't have many of the same doubts and worries as her mother. But far stronger was her desire to leave the sheltered existence she had always known and enter the world of action and adventure that Charles represented.

The young couple wanted to be married as soon as possible, but the Morrows insisted on a waiting period. Meanwhile, the media sensed something was up and began to keep a close watch on both the American embassy in Mexico City and the Morrows' mansion in Englewood. At last, on February 12, 1929, Ambassador Morrow confirmed the rumors of an engagement that had been circulating for weeks. But he refused to say when or where the wedding would take place.

The engagement was front-page news throughout the United States and in many other countries as well. In its wake the press began to keep an even closer watch on the comings and goings of Charles and the Morrows. When the family returned to its New Jersey home in the spring, reporters put the house under round-the-clock surveillance. They all wanted to be the first to break the story of the wedding.

Charles and Anne with her parents, Dwight and Betty Morrow, on a dock at the Morrows' summer vacation community in Maine. Corbis-Bettman.

Charles and his future mother-in-law devised an elaborate plan to outwit the reporters. On Sunday, May 26, 1929, Betty Morrow gave a reception in honor of Charles's mother, who was visiting the family and getting to know Anne. Reporters were stationed around the house, observing who entered and left through the front gate.

The next day there was less activity at the Morrow place, and the reporters relaxed their guard. Meanwhile, Mrs. Morrow phoned a few close friends and relatives and invited them to drop by that afternoon. By three fifteen, twenty-six guests were scattered throughout the downstairs rooms of the mansion, none of them aware that anything special was about to happen. Then Betty Morrow asked everyone to assemble in the living room.

Dr. William Brown, pastor of the church the Morrows attended, was waiting in front of the living-room fireplace. When the guests saw him, many finally guessed the reason for the gathering. After everyone was in place, a side door opened and Anne entered on the arm of her father. She wore a wedding gown of white chiffon, secretly made for her by the family's dressmaker. In her arms she carried a bouquet of larkspur and columbine her sister Elisabeth had picked in the garden that morning.

Anne came to stand beside Charles, dressed in a dark-blue suit, in front of Dr. Brown. There was no music, no best man, no maid of honor, and no photos were taken. Within minutes Dr. Brown had guided the couple through the marriage ceremony and Charles had put a plain gold wedding band on Anne's finger. Afterward the guests congratulated the bride and groom and the wedding cake was cut.

Charles and Anne did not stay long at the party. They excused themselves, went upstairs, and changed into the clothes they had worn earlier that day. Then, after hasty good-byes to Anne's parents, Charles's mother, and the other guests, they ducked down in the backseat of a friend's car and were driven away. None of the reporters waiting outside the gates spotted them.

On one of Englewood's back streets they climbed out of the friend's car and into Charles's, which another friend had brought to the rendezvous. Leaving New Jersey, they drove to an isolated spot on the Long Island shore, where a sleek new thirty-eight-foot motor launch, the *Mouette*, was lying at anchor. Charles had bought the boat for their honeymoon trip.

In the meantime Ambassador and Mrs. Morrow telephoned the major newspapers and press associations to let them know the wedding had taken place. The reporters waiting outside the Morrow home were informed of it via messages from their angry editors.

That night the newlyweds slipped out into Long Island Sound under cover of darkness and sailed up the coast toward Maine. For the next two days they enjoyed the peace and quiet of their privacy. But they were recognized when they docked at Block Island to refuel, and from then on reporters and photographers never left them alone.

Charles loads cans of fuel aboard his honeymoon yacht as a crowd of townspeople watches from the dock above. Library of Congress.

On June 6, as the *Mouette* neared York Harbor, Maine, they were buzzed by a press plane flying low with a photographer hanging out the window. Later, after Charles dropped anchor, a motorboat with another photographer on board approached their vessel. The photographer shouted at them to come up on deck for "just one picture," and when they refused, he circled the *Mouette* for seven straight hours, causing it to rock back and forth in the water.

At last, tired of the constant rocking, Charles gunned the *Mouette*'s engine. Turning away from their tormentor, he and Anne headed out toward open ocean, their anchor dragging along behind. They spent the night on a fishing bank, out of sight of land—and reporters.

Top: *Charles and Anne review the National Air Races in Cleveland, 1929.* National Air and Space Museum, Smithsonian Institution. Bottom: *The Lindberghs set off on a flight together, 1931.* Corbis-Bettman.

✧ CHAPTER FOURTEEN ✧

Lovers and Copilots

After their honeymoon was over, Anne entered wholeheartedly into Charles's aviation work. Together they traveled back and forth across the country, appearing at air shows, opening airports, and laying out the new TAT passenger route between New York and Los Angeles.

They had no home; instead they lived in hotels, on trains and planes, and in other people's houses. When they were in the New York area, they stayed with Anne's parents in Englewood or at the Morrows' apartment in New York City.

They had no private life, either. Charles's work demanded that he be constantly in the public eye, posing for photographers and giving interviews on the latest developments in aviation. But both he and Anne steadfastly refused to discuss their personal lives with the press. That, they continued to feel, was none of the public's business.

Occasionally, when they had a free day in New York, the Lindberghs would sneak out to a movie or for a walk in Central Park. To avoid being recognized, they assumed disguises. Charles would pull a cap down over his blond hair and put on eyeglass frames without lenses. Anne would wrap a scarf around her head and wear heavy makeup.

A few months after their wedding Charles began to give Anne flying lessons in a training plane that he had bought just for her. He was a demanding teacher. Most flying lessons lasted only half an hour; hers, which took place at the Long Island Aviation Club, were never less than an hour, and often much longer. Charles had her practice takeoffs and landings over and over again. But Anne was never heard to complain, or to ask for gentler treatment.

At last Charles judged she was ready for her first solo flight. Anne felt a thrill of exultation as she took off from the Aviation Club, flew over the towers of New York City, and made a smooth landing at Teterboro Airport in New Jersey.

Once she had mastered the basics of flying, Anne went on to study navigation. She also spent weeks learning how to operate the Morse code radios that were now standard equipment aboard most planes. With these skills in hand Anne became the navigator, radio operator, and copilot on Charles's longer flights.

In the open planes that they flew, Anne sat behind her husband in the passenger cockpit. There was too much noise for them to talk, but they could exchange notes from cockpit to cockpit. When they flew together, Charles treated Anne like a male partner. A newsreel photographer once caught the Lindberghs leaving their plane, with Anne—who was almost a foot shorter than her husband—coming second and carrying more than her share of the luggage.

Early in 1930 several New York newspapers confirmed the rumors that had been circulating for some time: The Lindberghs were expecting their first child. But this didn't stop Anne from flying. Charles had bought a Lockheed Sirius monoplane, and he and Anne planned to fly it nonstop at a high altitude from Los Angeles to New York. Lindbergh wanted to prove to the public that flying high above the weather was not only faster, but also safer and more comfortable than flying lower.

Anne was seven months pregnant when the Lindberghs took off from Los Angeles on Easter Sunday, 1930. Cruising at an altitude of 15,000 feet, the powerful Lockheed made the flight to New York in just fourteen hours and forty minutes. This was four hours less than the previous record.

The flight took its toll on Anne, however. Gasoline fumes from the plane's engine made her nauseous, and she was airsick and in pain the last four hours of the trip. She said nothing about it to Charles, not wanting to interrupt and possibly spoil their record flight.

When they landed at New York's Roosevelt Field, Charles met the waiting crowd of reporters and photographers by himself. Anne, still feeling ill, stayed behind in her cockpit until most of the newsmen had left. But several spotted her, looking pale and shaky, as she climbed into a limousine in her bulky flight suit. The next day some tabloid newspapers carried the untrue story that she had suffered a nervous breakdown.

A little more than two months later, on June 22, Anne gave birth to a son. It was also her twenty-fourth birthday. The Lindberghs sent a brief announcement of the birth to *The New York Times*, but true to form they gave no further details and refused to answer telephone inquiries.

As the days passed and the Lindberghs remained silent, rumors began to spread that something was wrong with the child. One rumor claimed that he was deformed, another that he had been born dead. At last, on July 9, Charles summoned the press to his downtown New York office. He announced that his son's name was Charles Augustus Lindbergh Jr., and he handed out a single baby picture that he had taken and developed himself.

Shortly after their son's birth, the Lindberghs moved into a rented farmhouse near Princeton, New Jersey. There they made plans for the home they were going to build in the Sourland Mountain region a few miles to the northwest. Charles had liked the look of the area when he flew over it, and had purchased 500 acres of wooded land. The site was three miles from the nearest village, Hopewell, and could be reached only by a narrow country road.

The United States was then in the midst of the Great Depression, following the collapse of the stock market the previous October, but the Lindberghs had not suffered any heavy losses in the crash. Consequently, they cut no corners in designing their new home. It was to be

Charles A. Lindbergh Jr. at seven months with, from left, his grandmother Betty Morrow, his great-grandmother Annie Cutter, and his mother, Anne. Library of Congress.

in the style of a French manor house, but constructed of native stone.

Besides planning the house and serving as an aviation consultant, Charles also wanted to pursue his scientific interests in some way. These dated all the way back to his boyhood, when he had worked alongside Grandfather Land in his Detroit laboratory.

A doctor friend told Charles of the studies being done by Dr. Alexis Carrel, head of the experimental surgery department at New York's Rockefeller Institute. Dr. Carrel believed that open-heart surgery and organ transplants—both of which seemed incredible in 1930—would one day be not only possible but commonplace. He was trying to develop a container in which organs could be kept alive and functioning outside the human body.

Charles arranged to meet Dr. Carrel, and the two men felt an immediate rapport. After the doctor described his experiments with glass pumps designed to preserve organs, and the problems he'd encountered with them, Charles said he'd like to try his hand at finding a solution. Carrel offered him a place in his laboratory, and Charles set to work with the same intensity he'd brought to building the *Spirit of St. Louis*.

In the spring of 1931, while they waited for their new home to be finished, Charles and Anne planned another flight. It would be the longest they had made together, and Charles's most ambitious journey since his solo flight to Paris. They would follow the so-called "northern circle route" from the United States to the Far East. It would take them up over Canada and Alaska, across the Bering Sea, then down to Russia's Kamchatka Peninsula and Japan, and on to their ultimate destination— China.

The flight was connected with Charles's job of exploring possible commercial air routes for Pan American Airlines, but he and Anne insisted on paying for it themselves. They planned to use the Lockheed Sirius monoplane they had flown nonstop from Los Angeles to New York the year before, and Anne would once again be the radio operator as well as copilot. Anne's mother agreed to look after little Charles Jr. while his parents were gone.

In late July the Lindberghs took off for Ottawa, Canada, and from there they flew north and west to the town of Churchill on the western shore of Hudson Bay. Traveling ever farther north, they went on to Baker Lake, crossed the Arctic Circle, and finally reached the tiny settlement of Aklavik on the Mackenzie River delta.

They flew beneath a pale sun that never set as the wooded wilderness below them gave way to flat, greenish-brown tundra. Because there were almost no airfields along their route, the Lindberghs' plane had been equipped with pontoons instead of wheels and needed a long stretch of open water in order to land safely. One danger after another threatened them: heavy fogs that completely enveloped their plane, high tides in Hudson Bay, miles of marsh and spongy ground where landings were impossible.

The regions of northern Canada over which they flew had few human inhabitants except for scattered groups of Eskimos and a handful of trappers, traders, mounted police, and missionaries. When the Lindberghs' plane came down in a lagoon or bay near one of the small, isolated settlements, the residents always welcomed them warmly. It wasn't often they had visitors from the world outside, especially someone famous like Lindbergh.

Leaving Canada, Charles and Anne flew to the northernmost point on their itinerary—Point Barrow, Alaska. Then they headed south once more, stopping at Nome, Alaska, before crossing the Bering Sea to Russia's Kamchatka Peninsula. From there they flew down over the Kuril Islands to Japan, and on to Nanking, China, a large city on the Yangtze River.

The Yangtze was in flood when the Lindberghs arrived, and the heavily populated valley through which it flowed had been transformed into a vast expanse of muddy water. Moved by the plight of the flood victims, the Lindberghs volunteered to make several flights over the affected area for China's National Flood Relief Commission. Flying low over the Yangtze, Charles and Anne surveyed how far its raging waters had reached and the damage they had done.

The Lindberghs after their arrival at Point Barrow, Alaska, the northernmost place they visited. Corbis-Bettman.

Chinese sailors help to get the Lindberghs' plane into the water for one of their mapping flights over the flooded Yangtze River. National Air and Space Museum, Smithsonian Institution.

Famine and epidemic diseases like cholera accompanied the flood and were killing thousands of Chinese. One day Charles flew a load of medical supplies to the walled city of Hinghwa, which was completely cut off by the flood. Crammed into the cockpit where Anne usually sat were two doctors—one Chinese and one American.

As soon as they landed on the river just outside the city walls, a dozen or more small boats filled with starving Chinese surrounded them. With gestures, Charles persuaded the owner of one of the boats to draw closer so that the Chinese doctor could unload the medical supplies into it.

When the hungry people watching in the other boats saw the bulky cardboard box, they thought it must contain food. They quickly clustered around the boat in which the doctor planned to deliver the medicines to the city, shouting and reaching out their arms. Hearing the commotion, Chinese in other boats on the river paddled over to find out what was going on. Soon a hundred or more vessels surrounded the doctor's boat and the plane.

The doctor realized there was no chance of his getting through to the city now. Leaving the medicines in the boat, he fought his way back to the plane. Some desperate Chinese, thinking there might be food aboard the plane also, tried to follow him onto the pontoons and fuselage.

Looking down on the scene, Charles was reminded of the mob that had crowded around the *Spirit of St. Louis* when he landed in Paris. But this situation was even more dangerous. The starving Chinese might damage the Sirius beyond repair or at the very least prevent it from taking off.

Charles reached for a .38 revolver that he carried in the cockpit. He held the gun high so the crowd could see it, then fired it over their heads in all directions. The Chinese got the message. They pulled away from the plane, and as soon as they had backed off far enough, Charles started the motor. The Sirius took off down the river, its mission sadly uncompleted. But at least Charles and the two doctors were safe.

A week later Charles had another narrow escape, this time with Anne. They had flown on to the city of Hankow, where the currents in the flooded Yangtze were even more treacherous than at Nanking. Fearful that the Sirius might be damaged if they anchored it in the river, the Lindberghs accepted an invitation from the captain of a British aircraft carrier to stow the plane on the carrier's deck.

One morning Charles and Anne were aboard the Sirius, ready to make their last survey flight over the Yangtze, when the crane that was lowering the plane into the river jammed. One of the plane's wings tipped down into the water, and the fast-flowing current pushed hard against it. It wouldn't be long before the pressure turned the plane over.

There was only one thing the Lindberghs could do if they didn't want to be trapped under the Sirius. "Jump!" yelled Charles, and he and Anne

Charles makes fast the lines to his capsized plane before it's hoisted out of the turbulent Yangtze. Library of Congress.

plunged into the river. They were swept downstream for several tense, frightening minutes before a lifeboat from the aircraft carrier picked them up. Miraculously neither of them was injured, but the Sirius had suffered extensive damage and would have to be shipped back to the United States.

Charles and Anne still hoped to visit the Chinese capital, Peking, before returning home. Then a cable came for Anne that made them change their plans. Her father, who had won election to the United States Senate the year before, had died of a stroke at his home in Englewood.

The Lindberghs booked immediate passage on an ocean liner bound from Shanghai to Seattle. It would be two years before they made another long flight in the repaired Sirius. Two years during which they would face a more challenging test than anything that had happened on their Pacific trip.

✧ CHAPTER FIFTEEN ✧

"They've Stolen Our Baby"

The last weekend in February 1932 was damp and chilly in New Jersey, and the Lindberghs' baby son caught a cold. His mother, Anne, felt achy and feverish, too.

As usual, the Lindberghs were spending the weekend at Highfields, their new home near the town of Hopewell. It had been finished the previous October, shortly after Charles's and Anne's return from the Far East, but the family had not moved in completely yet. From Monday to Friday they stayed with Anne's widowed mother at her mansion in Englewood. It was closer to Charles's office in New York City. Then, on Friday afternoons, they drove down to Highfields, returning to Englewood on Monday mornings.

This weekend was different, though. Because of the baby's cold and her own flu-ey feelings, Anne remained at Highfields on Monday while Charles drove directly into New York. Anne was expecting another child and didn't want to risk getting seriously ill. For company she had the Lindberghs' two live-in servants: the English butler, Oliver Whately, and his wife, Elsie, who served as cook and housekeeper.

Charles Jr. was better on Tuesday, but Anne decided to stay at Highfields one more day just to be on the safe side. She phoned Charles

Charles Lindbergh Jr. in a photo taken by his father in the fall of 1931.
UPI/Corbis-Bettman.

in New York to inform him of her change in plans. Next she called Englewood and asked the baby's nursemaid, Betty Gow, to come down and help her with Charles Jr. Betty looked after the child during the week, and Anne took care of him on weekends.

Betty arrived at Highfields about one twenty in the afternoon, driven by one of Mrs. Morrow's chauffeurs. In the meantime Charles went about his usual activities in New York that Tuesday. Just before five he phoned Anne to say he'd get to Highfields in a few hours, and to wait supper for him. At eight twenty-five or so he drove up the driveway and honked the car's horn to let her know he was home.

He didn't get to see Charles Jr. because Anne and Betty Gow had tucked him in earlier. Betty sat quietly with the child in his upstairs nursery until she was sure he was sound asleep, then latched the shutters on three of the four windows in the room. She couldn't latch the shutters on the fourth because they didn't close properly.

Shortly after Charles got home, Oliver Whately served him and Anne a light supper. Afterward they were sitting by the fire in the living room when they heard a crash that sounded, Charles said later, "like the slats from a crate falling off a chair." He thought the sound came from the kitchen, but it wasn't loud enough to make him go and investigate.

A few minutes later Charles and Anne went upstairs. He took a bath, then came back down to the library to read a book. Anne drew a bath for herself after Charles had finished. Neither of them looked in on their sleeping son.

At ten Betty Gow checked on Charles Jr. as she always did at that hour. She did not turn on a lamp but relied on the light coming through the open door as she crossed the room and switched on an electric heater. Then she went over to the baby's bed to make sure he was sleeping peacefully. But he wasn't there.

Thinking Anne might have him, Betty hurried to her mistress's room and found Anne coming out of the bathroom. No, she hadn't had him, Anne said.

Told that Charles was in the library, Betty raced downstairs to see if he had taken the child.

When Charles learned that the baby wasn't in his crib, he rushed up to the nursery with Betty behind him. Anne was already there, peering under the bed in the vain hope that Charles Jr. was playing hide-and-seek. Together she and Charles stared at the empty crib, and he said, "Anne, they've stolen our baby."

Looking about the room, they saw that the southeast corner window—the one with the shutters that wouldn't close—was wide open. On the sill was an envelope. Charles was about to reach for it when he noticed a muddy footprint on the floor beneath the window. Other muddy spots led from the window to the crib.

Pulling himself together, Charles told Oliver Whately to call the

Hopewell police department and said the envelope should not be opened until the police examined it for fingerprints. Anne and Betty Gow searched the rest of the upstairs rooms while Charles himself made two calls. The first was to the New Jersey state police, the second to his friend and lawyer, Colonel Henry Breckinridge, in New York City.

The calls completed, Charles took a rifle from his bedroom closet and went out into the dark, windy night. He walked for about a hundred yards up the driveway until he realized it was pointless. Without a flashlight, he wouldn't be able to spot even the most obvious clues. Frustrated, he turned back toward Highfields to wait for the arrival of the police.

The local chief of police and his deputy got there first. They were followed by thirteen state police officials, including Colonel H. Norman Schwarzkopf (father of the general who led American ground forces in the 1991 Gulf War).

The local and state policemen explored the grounds around the house by flashlight. Under the southeast corner window of the nursery they found a three-quarter-inch chisel. Nearby in the muddy earth were a man's footprints leading away from the house. The policemen followed the prints for a distance of about seventy-five feet and came upon a folding ladder that the kidnaper had apparently abandoned.

The ladder was built of odds and ends of lumber and consisted of three sections, each of them seven feet long. The policemen noted that one of the rungs in the bottom section was broken. When Charles was told of it, he guessed that the sound of the rung cracking was what he'd heard while talking to Anne after supper.

Back at the house a police expert examined the envelope in the nursery for fingerprints, but found none. With only Charles and a few top officials present he opened the envelope and read the note inside:

> Dear Sir!
>   Have 50,000$ redy 25,000$ in 20$ bills 15,000$ in 10$ bills and 10,000$ in 5$ bills. After 2–4 days we will inform

you were to deliver the Mony.

We warn you for making anyding public or for the Polise the child is in gut care.

Indication for all letters are singnature and 3 holds.

The "singnature" was made up of two interlocking blue circles, shaded in red where they overlapped. Three square holes pierced the design.

After the reading was over, Colonel Schwarzkopf's chief aide turned to Charles and asked: "Now, whom do you want to see this note, Colonel?" By doing so, he in effect turned control of the case over to Charles—a move that would cause confusion later. For the goals of the police and the Lindberghs were not always the same.

From the first the police wanted above all to bring the kidnaper or kidnapers to justice, while the Lindberghs' chief concern was the safe return of their baby son. In line with that aim Charles insisted that the contents of the ransom note be kept from the public as the writer of the note had demanded.

Within the hour the first newspaper reporters and photographers

Air view of Highfields, the Lindberghs' estate in New Jersey. Charles Jr. was kidnaped through the last upstairs window in the wing at the left. UPI/Corbis-Bettman.

arrived at Highfields. For once Charles welcomed them warmly, thinking he and Anne might be able to communicate with the kidnapers through the press. Oliver Whately served the reporters coffee and sandwiches while Anne provided them with information about the baby's diet and other things the kidnapers would need to know in order to care for her son.

The Lindberghs' honeymoon with the press didn't last long. By noon the next day hundreds of reporters had descended on the village of Hopewell to cover what many called "the biggest news story since the stock market crash." The reporters swarmed around the Lindberghs' three-car garage where Colonel Schwarzkopf had set up his headquarters and roamed at will through the woods and fields surrounding the house.

On the evening of March 2 Charles held a press conference. During it he said he and Anne would give out no news directly from now on because it might interfere with efforts to recover their son. Instead, he would arrange for the media to obtain information from other sources about any new developments in the case. He asked the reporters to leave Hopewell, and most of them agreed to do so.

But the public was still fascinated by the kidnaping, so the press kept up its steady coverage. The Associated Press and the United Press daily sent out more than 10,000 words about the case to their wire service subscribers. To feed this flow the smallest revelations were made to seem important, rumors were reported as facts, and some so-called "news stories" were nothing but fiction.

Everyone connected with the Lindberghs suffered from the unending publicity. Charles's mother was besieged by reporters as she continued to teach her high school chemistry classes in Detroit. Anne's younger sister, Constance, who was attending Smith College, and her brother, Dwight Jr., who was at Amherst, were put under special police protection after they complained of being hounded by reporters.

The police closely questioned the Lindberghs' servants and those at the Morrow mansion because they thought the crime might be, at least

Reporters and newsreel cameramen gather in Hopewell, New Jersey, to cover the Lindbergh kidnaping. Corbis-Bettman.

in part, an inside job. How else would the kidnapers have known that the Lindberghs were still at Highfields on that Tuesday night, when always before they had returned to Englewood on Monday? And how would they have known which window in the baby's nursery had a broken shutter?

When the press got wind of the questioning, they made the lives of some of the servants miserable. Betty Gow, for example, had been dating a Norwegian sailor named Red Johnson. Learning that he was a suspect, the press labeled Johnson "the mysterious foreigner" in the case and kept on running stories about the sailor long after he had proved his innocence.

The continuing press coverage made it more difficult for Charles to get in touch with the kidnapers. He received a second ransom note on March 5, signed with the same interlocking circles. It criticized him for having told the police about the first note, and asked: "Is it realy necessary to make a world affair out off this?" It also raised the ransom demand from $50,000 to $70,000.

In their eagerness to get their son back the Lindberghs issued a statement saying they would be willing to work with any and all go-betweens, even representatives of organized crime. There had been speculation that the baby had been kidnaped by one of the big-city gangs, such as Al Capone's mob in Chicago, that dominated the American crime scene at the time.

Worried that the Lindberghs' statement might be misinterpreted, the attorney general of New Jersey issued a statement of his own. It said that the state's law enforcement officers could not be bound by any promises of immunity Charles and Anne made to the kidnapers.

At this point an unlikely go-between phoned the Lindbergh residence. He was not a representative of organized crime but a seventy-two-year-old retired teacher from the Bronx, Dr. John F. Condon.

Like many Americans, Dr. Condon thought Charles Lindbergh was the nation's greatest living hero. When he heard about the kidnaping, Condon wanted to do something to help his hero at this time of crisis. The retired teacher gave an interview to the *Bronx Home News* in which he said he would gladly add his life savings of $1,000 to the Lindberghs' reported ransom offer of $50,000.

Condon also said he was ready, at his own expense, to go anywhere to give the kidnapers the extra money, and he promised never to divulge their identities to anyone. Now Dr. Condon was phoning Charles because, two days after the interview appeared, Condon had received a crudely written response to his offer.

Lindbergh and his lawyer were skeptical at first, thinking Condon was probably just another of the hundreds who had called with what proved to be false leads. But when Condon mentioned that the note was signed with two interlocking circles, they invited him to bring it down to New Jersey that very night. No one except those closest to the investigation knew that the other ransom notes had been signed with similar circles.

✧ CHAPTER SIXTEEN ✧

"That Is My Son"

Driven by two friends, Dr. Condon didn't reach Highfields until two A.M., but Charles and his lawyer were waiting for him. They examined the note he brought, which was obviously written in the same handwriting as the earlier ones and contained similar spelling errors.

The note repeated the demand for a ransom of $70,000. After Dr. Condon had obtained it from Charles, the note said, he should take out a three-word ad in *The New York American*: "Money is ready." Then Condon should plan to be at home every night between six and twelve. Sometime during those hours he would hear from the kidnapers.

Dr. Condon stayed overnight at Highfields, and the next day Charles and his lawyer drove him back to his home in the Bronx. Charles had disguised himself for the trip and was carrying a suitcase containing $70,000 in cash. He had raised the first $50,000 by selling most of his aviation stocks, and had obtained the remaining $20,000 via a bank loan.

Condon's three-word message to the kidnapers appeared in the March 11 issue of *The New York American*. To keep his identity a secret from any reporters who might spot the notice, Condon had signed it with a code name, "Jafsie." It came from his initials, J.F.C.

That evening at seven Condon's phone rang. The hoarse-voiced male caller said simply, "I saw your ad in *The American*." He told Condon to be at home on the following evening, when he would receive another message, and then the caller hung up.

Condon immediately informed Charles of the call, and the next night he and his lawyer were waiting with Condon in his living room when the doorbell rang. It was a cabdriver, delivering a note from the kidnapers. The note directed Condon to go to an empty frankfurter stand at the end of a subway line in the north Bronx.

The retired teacher followed the note's instructions, but he did not take the ransom money with him. At the frankfurter stand Condon found a second note that told him to go down the street to the gates of Woodlawn Cemetery and wait outside for a signal.

Condon did so, and soon he saw someone waving a white handkerchief in the dark shadows of the cemetery. The teacher opened his arms wide to show he was unarmed, and a moment later a slender man in his late thirties emerged from the darkness. The man's overcoat collar was drawn up over the lower part of his face, and his hat was pulled down over his forehead.

"Did you got it, the money?" the man asked in a German accent.

Condon said no, explaining that Colonel Lindbergh had to be sure the man really represented the kidnapers before any money was turned over. He persuaded the man—who said his name was John—to walk with him to a nearby park. There they sat on a bench and continued their conversation.

John told Condon that he represented a gang of five, three men and two women. He said the gang was holding the baby on a boat but refused to give even a hint of its location. At first he assured Condon that Charles Jr. was safe and well. Then he startled the teacher by asking suddenly, "What if the baby is dead? Would I burn if the baby is dead?"

"Not if you had no part in it," Condon replied. He went on to tell John that the Lindberghs wanted definite proof that he and his partners actually had the child. The police had given reporters a false description of Charles Jr.'s sleeping suit as a way of checking the claims of people who sought a ransom for his return. Now Dr. Condon asked John to send him the garment the baby had been wearing when he was taken from his crib.

After thinking for a moment, John said that was no problem—he would arrange to have the suit sent to Condon in a few days. The men parted, and four days later a package wrapped in brown paper arrived by mail at the Condon residence. Inside was a Dr. Denton's sleeping suit, freshly laundered. Charles drove in at once from New Jersey to examine the suit and said it appeared to be his son's.

Later, at Highfields, Anne confirmed the identification, after bursting into tears when Charles spread out the little suit in front of her. But she remained hopeful. "They keep assuring me that the baby is safe and will be returned," she wrote to her mother-in-law. "But we must play a game of patience."

For a week Condon ran an ad in *The New York American*: "I accept. The package is delivered and is okay. Money is ready." But no response came from the man Condon and Charles had begun to call Graveyard John. Meanwhile, Charles's bank put together a new package of ransom money to replace the first one. This time the serial number of every bill was recorded, and a number of gold certificates were included. The certificates—similar to dollar bills, but with some easily recognizable differences—were about to be withdrawn from circulation. Thus they would be easier to trace when the kidnapers cashed them in.

In addition, the agents wanted to mark each bill. At first Charles objected: In their appeals to the kidnapers he and Anne had said they weren't interested in prosecuting the criminals, only in getting their son back alive. If the bills were marked, that promise would be broken. He withdrew his objection only after the federal agents working on the case threatened to leave unless the ransom was paid with marked money.

On March 31 a letter finally came from Graveyard John. It set Saturday night, April 2, as the date for the payment of the ransom. On that night Charles was waiting with Condon in the latter's living room when a cabdriver once again delivered a message from John. It gave Condon preliminary directions on where to go with the money.

Charles strapped a .38 pistol under his suit jacket in case there was trouble. Then he himself drove Condon to the place in the east Bronx that John had designated. Between them on the car's front seat rested a wooden box containing the $70,000 ransom.

At their destination, a darkened greenhouse, Condon found another note under a stone. It told him to go up the road until he came to St. Raymond's Cemetery. Charles decided it would be best if Condon left the money in the car and went to the cemetery by himself. Then, after confirming that John was there, he could come back for the ransom.

Condon agreed to this plan, got out of the car, and walked slowly and cautiously to the cemetery. He paced back and forth in front of the entrance for a few minutes, then shouted to Charles, "There doesn't seem to be anybody here!"

In response, a voice came out of the darkness that Lindbergh heard clearly from the car. "Hey, doctor!" it called in a heavy German accent. "Over here, doctor!"

Condon entered the cemetery and found John crouched behind a hedge near the entrance. John asked Condon if he had the money, and the old man said yes—but he wanted a "receipt" disclosing the whereabouts of the baby before he turned it over. On impulse, he told John the ransom would be the amount originally demanded, $50,000 not $70,000.

John protested loudly but eventually agreed to the lower figure, as Condon had guessed he would. He also promised to give Condon a note telling where the baby was.

Pleased with himself for having saved the Lindberghs some money, Condon returned to the car. Charles removed a packet containing $20,000 from the box and Condon carried the rest back to John, who had stayed behind in the cemetery.

John opened the box to make sure the $50,000 was really inside it. Then he handed Condon a sealed envelope. "Don't open it yet," he warned. "Wait for six hours."

Back at the car Condon was surprised when Charles refused to open the envelope at once. Perhaps, as with the marked bills, he felt he must play by the criminals' rules to insure the safety of his son. But he was too anxious to know the note's contents to wait six hours. Stopping the car alongside a children's playground, Charles ripped open the envelope.

The boy was on a boat called *Nelly*, the note began. It told Charles he would find the boat between Horseneck Beach and Gay Head on Elizabeth Island.

The island was in Long Island Sound, off the shore of Connecticut. Charles knew the area well; he and Anne had sailed around the island on their honeymoon. The next day Charles took off in a borrowed seaplane from Bridgeport, Connecticut, and flew back and forth over the shoreline of Connecticut and Rhode Island, searching for a boat named the *Nelly*. But there was no sign of it.

He searched for two whole days, dipping low over the Sound when he spotted a boat that seemed to fit the *Nelly*'s description. At last he had to admit that there was no such boat. He had been duped by the kidnapers. He had paid Graveyard John $50,000 for nothing.

But he and Anne still didn't give up hope. "We have had some very disappointing setbacks," Anne wrote to Charles's mother in Detroit on April 6. "But the consensus is that the child is still safe and well."

Dr. Condon didn't give up hope, either. In the next few days he placed more ads, saying "What is wrong? Have you crossed me? Please send better instructions." He got no response from John, but reporters noticed the ads, guessed what was behind them, and published their conclusions.

Since contact with John had been broken, Charles and his advisers decided there was no point in denying the stories. It was announced that Charles had indeed paid a ransom to a mysterious Graveyard John, using an intermediary known as "Jafsie." At once Dr. Condon became a celebrity. He was questioned for hours by detectives and interviewed by countless newspapermen and radio reporters.

Dr. John F. "Jafsie" Condon at the right. With him is New Jersey Attorney General David T. Wilentz.
UPI/Corbis-Bettman.

At this point a fresh lead surfaced. John Hughes Curtis, a boatbuilder in Norfolk, Virginia, said he had been approached by the kidnapers in late March and had met with them on a boat in Chesapeake Bay in April. He even claimed to have seen some of the ransom money.

Colonel Schwarzkopf didn't believe Curtis's story and advised Charles to have nothing to do with the man. But by this time Charles was ready to follow up any lead, however unlikely it might be. He joined Curtis in Virginia, and the two men set out to sea in a borrowed yacht. They were searching for the fishing vessel on which Curtis said the kidnapers were holding the child.

Charles was still at sea on May 12 when a truck stopped along the lonely road between Hopewell and Princeton in New Jersey. Needing to relieve himself, the driver walked into the woods the road cut through. There he stumbled onto the badly decomposed body of a baby, buried under a thin cover of leaves and dirt. The spot was less than two miles from the Lindberghs' home, Highfields.

The man reported his discovery to the police, and they in turn notified Anne, who was staying at Highfields with her mother and Betty Gow. Anne took the news calmly, but she did not go to the funeral home to identify the remains. That painful chore fell to Betty Gow and the child's pediatrician.

Charles Jr. was still wearing a flannel undershirt that Betty recognized as one she had sewn for him. The pediatrician made a positive identification based on the child's teeth and hair. An autopsy revealed that he had died from a blow to his skull just above the left forehead. The location of the burial and the condition of the remains indicated that death had probably occurred almost immediately after he was kidnaped.

When Anne was told the details, she wrote in her diary that she felt "strangely a sense of peace. . . . It is a relief to know that he did not live beyond that night."

Charles didn't hear of his son's fate until the yacht put in to shore that evening. "Colonel," one of the men on the dock told him, "your baby has been—found."

"Found?" Lindbergh said. "You mean—"

"He is dead," the man replied.

Charles returned at once to New Jersey, taking John Curtis with him. He wanted to find out whether Curtis had been telling him the truth. The two men arrived at Highfields in the early hours of Friday, May 13, and later that morning Charles insisted on being taken to the funeral home. He had to be sure, he said, that the remains were really those of his son.

Outside the funeral home he shoved his way through a crowd of onlookers and reporters shouting questions. Once inside, he was led to a room where a small body lay on a table, covered by a sheet. Charles asked that the sheet be removed, and he stood there for a few seconds, his face turning red as he looked down.

"Yes," he said at last. "That is my son."

✦ CHAPTER SEVENTEEN ✦

Another Flight . . . and an Arrest

Somehow two newspaper photographers managed to get into the funeral home where Charles Jr. lay and took pictures of his remains. The photos were too horrible to publish, but prints turned up for sale at various places in New Jersey, going for five dollars each.

Charles and Anne were stunned when they learned of these "coffin shots." They hadn't been able to safeguard their son in life; now they couldn't even protect him in death. Fearing that his funeral might turn into a mob scene, and his grave would become a tourist attraction, they decided on immediate cremation. A few weeks later Charles scattered the ashes over the Atlantic from the window of a plane.

Once the baby's body was identified, John Curtis confessed to the police that he had made up the story that had lured Charles to Virginia. He had hoped, Curtis said, to sell it to the newspapers and raise enough money to pay his gambling debts. Charged with obstruction of justice, Curtis was eventually tried and sentenced to a year in jail.

Meanwhile, the police subjected the Lindbergh and Morrow servants to new and intense rounds of questioning. They were more convinced than ever that someone on the thirty-two-person staff at Mrs. Morrow's

The hearse bearing the remains of Charles Jr. is surrounded by curious onlookers as it leaves the funeral home in Trenton on its way to the crematorium.
UPI/Corbis-Bettman.

mansion had links to the kidnapers. And Charles shared their suspicions.

The police focused their attentions at first on Harry Ellerson, the assistant chauffeur who had driven Betty Gow down to Highfields on the day of the kidnaping. But Ellerson had an airtight alibi; several witnesses had seen him that evening at a bar in Fort Lee, New Jersey, not far from the Morrow estate.

Next, the police and Charles turned the spotlight on Violet Sharpe, a young Englishwoman who worked as a downstairs maid at the mansion. When investigated earlier, Violet had told first one story and then another about where she'd been the night of the kidnaping. Now she admitted she'd fed information about the family's reaction to the crime to a reporter from the *New York Daily News*. But she claimed that had nothing to do with the sudden increase in the size of her bank account.

Summoned to yet another round of questioning, the young woman panicked. She swallowed poison and died in the kitchen pantry of the Morrow mansion before she could be revived. Her suicide caused a scandal, especially after those she'd been with on the night of the kidnaping confirmed the second story she'd told investigators.

The tabloid press blamed Violet Sharpe's death on the New Jersey state police's use of "brutal third-degree tactics," as one paper put it. Charles felt differently. He had been present at the questionings and knew they had been conducted quite gently. If anyone was to blame, he and Anne thought it was the press, which had engaged in all sorts of lurid speculations about Sharpe's love life.

Whoever was responsible, Violet Sharpe's suicide effectively ended the investigation of the servants. Neither the Lindberghs nor Mrs. Morrow wanted people who were probably innocent to be harassed unnecessarily. As a result, it was never known whether someone in the Morrow household—perhaps even Violet—had aided the kidnapers.

On August 16, 1932, Anne gave birth to the Lindberghs' second son at her mother's spacious apartment in New York City. Charles had felt it would be easier to maintain security at the apartment than in a hospital. He was present when the baby was born, and together he and Anne decided on the boy's name: Jon Morrow.

After announcing the birth, Charles released a statement to the press. "Mrs. Lindbergh and I have made our home in New Jersey," he said. "It is naturally our wish to continue to live there near our friends and interests. Obviously, however, it is impossible for us to subject our second son to the publicity which we feel was in large measure responsible for the death of our first."

He ended with a plea. "We feel that our children have a right to grow up normally with other children. Continued publicity will make this impossible. I am appealing to the press to permit our children to live the lives of normal Americans."

Unfortunately, Charles's plea had no effect on the tabloid newspapers. To satisfy the curiosity of their readers, the papers continued to print every item they could dig up about the activities of the Lindberghs and their newborn son. As a consequence the family's mail increased dramatically, and Charles and Anne began to get letters threatening to kidnap Jon.

Before the baby's birth the Lindberghs had left Highfields, and they were now living full-time in a suite of rooms in Mrs. Morrow's mansion. To protect Jon, Charles hired special watchmen for the estate and bought a guard dog, a fierce-looking German shepherd whom they named Thor. But the animal was gentle with those he knew, especially the baby.

Life for the Lindberghs gradually returned to something like normalcy in the months after Jon's birth. Charles resumed his consulting work for the airlines and plunged back into the scientific experiments he was conducting with Dr. Alexis Carrel at the Rockefeller Institute. Anne started to write her first book, *North to the Orient*, a poetic account of the Lindberghs' 1931 flight to the Far East.

As 1932 ended and 1933 began, marked bills from the ransom payment showed up occasionally at banks in the New York City area. The police were not able to trace any of them, however. In May, when all gold certificates remaining in circulation had to be surrendered, a teller at the Federal Reserve Bank in New York discovered that he had taken in $2,980 worth of certificates from the ransom.

The teller had been so busy all day that he had failed to notice who had presented the certificates, but he did have an exchange receipt signed by a J. J. Faulkner. The police hurried to the New York address on the receipt, only to come up against a dead end. No one named Faulkner lived there.

By the late spring of 1933 Charles and Anne realized they could never again feel safe or comfortable living at Highfields. The house and

Top: *Anne in the cockpit of the Lockheed Sirius during the Lindberghs' 30,000-mile survey flight around the northern Atlantic, 1933. Bottom: Friendly inhabitants welcome Charles and Anne to Greenland, the third stop on their Atlantic flight.* Both photos from the National Air and Space Museum, Smithsonian Institution.

grounds held too many dark memories for them. They donated the property to a nonprofit foundation that they had established themselves. The foundation would set up and operate a home for children at Highfields "without discrimination in regard to race or creed."

In the summer of 1933 the Lindberghs embarked on their longest air journey yet. Their mission: to explore possible northern and southern air routes across the Atlantic, as a step toward the establishment of regular passenger flights. Jon, now almost a year old, would stay at the Morrow family's summer home in Maine while his parents were away. Looking after him would be Grandmother Lindbergh, assisted by Betty Gow and a squad of armed guards hired by Charles.

The Lindberghs left New York on July 9, flying the same Lockheed Sirius seaplane that had taken them to the Orient two years earlier. They headed north to Nova Scotia and then on to Labrador and Greenland, where they made a special scientific survey of the microscopic life in the air above the icecap. Anne operated the radio most of the time, but sometimes she flew the plane, which was equipped with dual controls.

At a port in Greenland a young boy climbed up on one of the wings and painted a name on the fuselage. It was what everyone in his country called the plane: *Tingmissartoq*, meaning "the one who flies like a big bird" in Inuit. Charles and Anne were delighted with the name and left it on the plane.

From Greenland the Lindberghs flew east to Iceland, then down to the Faeroe and Shetland Islands, and on to Denmark. They paid visits to Sweden and Finland, and received tremendous welcomes at Leningrad and Moscow in the Soviet Union. Turning west again, they stopped briefly in Norway, then flew to the British Isles, where Anne had a joyous reunion with her sister Elisabeth, who had married the year before and was now living in Wales.

Continuing their European tour, the Lindberghs flew to France and Holland, then on to Switzerland, Spain, and Portugal. After stops at the Azores and Canary Islands in the Atlantic, they headed south for the

Cape Verde Islands. From there they hoped to take off for Brazil, but strong headwinds and high ocean breakers prevented it. Instead they flew back to Gambia, on the west coast of Africa, where they waited a week for a strong-enough tailwind. At last, after discarding more than two hundred pounds of supplies, they managed to get the *Tingmissartoq* into the air.

The nonstop flight across the South Atlantic took seventeen and a half hours, and by the time the Lindberghs landed in Natal, Brazil, Anne was more than ready to head on home. It was now early December, they had been gone for more than five months, and she missed Jon terribly. But Charles was eager, as he said, "for new adventures." Rather than take the shortest air route from Brazil to the United States, he wanted to fly up the Amazon River to the city of Manaus before turning north.

Why was Charles seemingly reluctant to return to America? Perhaps he wanted to put off becoming involved again in the hunt for the kidnapers, and all the painful memories that would bring back. Or perhaps he simply wanted to stay up in the air a little longer. High above the earth and sea, away from the prying eyes of reporters, was the only place Lindbergh felt truly free.

Whatever his motives, Charles got his way. He and Anne flew a leisurely route north via Trinidad, Puerto Rico, and the Dominican Republic. They didn't arrive in New York until December 19, just in time to spend Christmas week with Jon.

In January 1934 the Lindberghs moved into a small penthouse apartment in New York City—the first home of their own they'd had since leaving Highfields. They hoped to stay out of the limelight for a while, but the very next month Charles found himself thrust back into the news.

President Franklin D. Roosevelt had issued an executive order suspending all airmail contracts with the commercial airlines that had been carrying the mail up till now. Until new contracts were awarded, the U.S. Army Air Corps would fly the mail. This followed a congressional investigation that revealed that the existing contracts had been given to the nation's largest and most powerful airlines, regardless of whether or not they had submitted the lowest bids.

Upon hearing the news, Charles sent a telegram to President Roosevelt protesting his action. Suspending the contracts, Charles wrote, "condemns the largest portion of our commercial aviation without trial." Remembering his own experiences flying the mail, Charles also feared for the safety of the army pilots who had been assigned the job—many of them had no training in night flying.

The telegram and Charles's later testimony before a congressional committee revealed his political naiveté. He simply couldn't believe that the executives of the major airlines, many of whom he knew personally, would use unfair or illegal methods to obtain government contracts. If someone was his friend, he assumed that person played by the same rules he used, when in fact many executives did not.

On the other hand, Charles was right when it came to flying safety. In the first week after the Army Air Corps took over the mail, five pilots died in crashes and six others were seriously injured. By the end of March the pilot death toll had risen to twelve. An aroused public joined Charles in protesting this turn of events, and President Roosevelt was forced to withdraw his order and return the airmail to the companies that had been carrying it before.

Republicans in Congress and throughout the country were delighted. Since taking office in March 1933, President Roosevelt had had his way with almost all his programs and policies. Now Charles Lindbergh had forced the president to retreat on the airmail issue. Some Republicans hoped that Lindbergh might be persuaded to run for president against Roosevelt in 1936, even thought Charles claimed that he had no political ambitions.

As for Roosevelt, he was not a man to take defeat lightly. Nor did he forget or forgive the actions of those who opposed him on what he felt were unjust grounds. These qualities of Roosevelt's would cause serious problems for Lindbergh later on. But in the spring of 1934, with the airmail back in private hands, Charles quietly savored his victory over the president.

Life was more relaxed for the Lindberghs that summer. Charles tested a new high-wing seaplane for Sikorsky Aircraft while Anne continued work on her book and wrote a long article for *National Geographic* about their Atlantic flights the year before. In September the Lindberghs were vacationing on the comedian Will Rogers's California ranch when a call came that destroyed their holiday mood. A suspect in the kidnaping had been arrested, they were told. His name was Bruno Richard Hauptmann.

Anne shuddered when she heard the news. "It's starting all over again!" she exclaimed. But Charles felt a surge of hope and made plans for their immediate return to New York.

CHAPTER EIGHTEEN

"The Trial of the Century"

Several days after his return Charles disguised himself with sunglasses and a plain cloth cap and went to the Bronx County district attorney's office. There he sat amid a group of federal and state agents as the prisoner, Bruno Hauptmann, was brought in. Later, Charles described Hauptmann as a well-built, good-looking man. But his eyes were small and shifty, Lindbergh said, like the eyes of a wild boar.

Charles watched and listened intently as Hauptmann, following an agent's instructions, walked back and forth across the front of the room. As he walked, the prisoner called out the words Graveyard John had shouted to Dr. Condon the night the ransom was paid. "Hey, doctor! Over here, doctor!"

After the guards had taken Hauptmann away, the agents asked Charles for his reactions. He told them he would be willing to swear that Hauptmann's voice was the one he had heard calling out from the Bronx cemetery on the night of April 2, 1932.

The discovery and arrest of Bruno Richard Hauptmann had come about partly by luck and partly as a result of careful detective work. On September 15, 1934, a gas station attendant in New York City sold five gallons of gasoline to a man who paid for it with a gold certificate. The attendant noted that the man had a heavy German accent.

As the customer pulled away from the gas pump, the attendant jotted down his license number on the gold certificate. All gas station workers in the city had been asked to do so by the agents investigating the kidnaping. Later the attendant took the certificate to a nearby bank, where it was identified as one of the Lindbergh bills.

The police checked the license number and discovered that the car's owner was a German-born carpenter named Bruno Richard Hauptmann who lived in the Bronx with his wife, Anna, and infant son, Mannfried. Agents staked out Hauptmann's house, stopped him when he left it, and found another certificate from the ransom in his wallet. This gave the agents enough evidence to arrest Hauptmann and hold him for questioning. A few days later Charles identified his voice as the one he had heard calling out from the Bronx cemetery.

As the police pursued their investigation further, they unearthed a great deal of information about Bruno Hauptmann's past. Born in 1899 and a veteran of World War I, he had lived in the United States for almost twelve years. He had arrived in New York as a stowaway in 1923 after escaping from a German prison, where he was awaiting trial for a series of burglaries.

With the help of other German immigrants, Hauptmann found work in machine shops and on construction projects. He married a hardworking German woman, Anna Schoeffler, and together they amassed a nest egg of $25,000. But Hauptmann lost it all in 1931 through bad stock market investments.

The police learned that Hauptmann had worked only off and on during the winter of 1931–32. However, he began making large deposits in a savings account starting in April 1932. This was shortly after Charles paid the ransom to Graveyard John.

The trial of Bruno Richard Hauptmann for the kidnaping and murder of Charles A. Lindbergh Jr. began on January 2, 1935. That morning thousands of people crowded into the small New Jersey town of Flemington where the trial was being held. They surrounded the courthouse, hoping to get inside, but only a hundred or so seats were

Bruno Hauptmann, handcuffed to two detectives, enters the Bronx County Courthouse for questioning, September 20, 1934. UPI/Corbis-Bettman.

Top: *Charles Lindbergh leaves his limousine to attend the opening day of Bruno Hauptmann's trial, January 5, 1935.* Bottom: *Anne Lindbergh approaches the courthouse on the morning she is scheduled to testify. Following behind are her mother, in black coat, accompanied by Mrs. Norman Schwarzkopf Sr.* Both photos from UPI/Corbis-Bettman.

available to the public. The rest were reserved for those involved with the case and members of the press. Nearly two hundred reporters came from as far away as Germany and China to cover what was called "the trial of the century."

The citizens of Flemington made the most of their town's sudden fame. Every room in the Union Hotel had been booked for months, and rooms in private homes were renting for huge amounts. Drugstore soda fountains featured items called the "Lindbergh sundae" and the "Hauptmann pudding." Instead of selling lemonade, two enterprising boys snipped off their little brother's curls and advertised them as "genuine locks of hair from the Lindbergh baby." The price for a lock: twenty-five cents.

Charles attended the court proceedings undisguised. He sat alone, watching as the jury was chosen. Each prospective juror was questioned at length by the prosecutor, David T. Wilentz, and Hauptmann's chief defense attorney, Edward J. Reilly.

Anne joined her husband on January 5, when she was scheduled to appear as the second witness for the prosecution. She had to identify her son's clothing and describe the events of the night he was kidnaped, and she did so in a quiet, controlled manner. The defense did not cross-examine her.

Charles was the next witness. He, too, had to relive all the events of that terrible night, from the noise he had heard while he and Anne were sitting in the living room to the moment when Betty Gow told him the baby was missing. Then the prosecutor led Charles through everything that had happened after that, including his trip to the cemetery with Dr. Condon, when he heard a voice with a foreign accent call out, "Hey, doctor!"

"Since that time, have you heard the same voice?" Prosecutor Wilentz asked.

"Yes, I have," said Charles. "It was Hauptmann's voice."

Hauptmann's attorney, Edward Reilly, went on the attack immediately when he cross-examined Charles. He tried to throw suspicion on the Lindbergh and Morrow servants, but Charles reminded him that the police had failed to turn up incriminating evidence against any of them.

As the trial proceeded, the circumstantial evidence against Hauptmann mounted higher day by day. Police experts traced the lumber from which the handmade ladder used in the kidnaping was made to a mill in North Carolina. A store in the Bronx had stocked a supply of this lumber, and their records showed that Bruno Hauptmann had bought a sizable amount of it in December 1931, three months before the kidnaping. Even more damaging, a board found in Hauptmann's attic proved, under microscopic examination, to have once been of a piece with a rung in the kidnap ladder.

Handwriting tests also pointed toward Hauptmann's guilt. All of the ransom notes, including the one left on the windowsill in Charles Jr.'s nursery, matched samples of Hauptmann's handwriting. And when he wrote, from dictation, test words taken from the notes, he made the same spelling errors that the kidnaper had.

In addition the police had found a large part of the ransom payment hidden in Hauptmann's garage. Bills and certificates totaling $14,950 were concealed under the floor and in hollowed-out beams in the walls and roof. Hauptmann claimed that this money had been given to him for safekeeping by a former business partner, Isidor Fisch, before the man returned to Germany.

The police sought out Fisch to confirm Hauptmann's story, only to discover that he had died of tuberculosis in March 1934. German officials told the police that Fisch was penniless at the time of his death, and thus could not afford the medical treatment that might have saved his life. Why then, the police wondered, had Fisch left so much money with Hauptmann? It didn't make sense—and turned out to be yet another piece of incriminating evidence against the accused.

Most crucial of all, Hauptmann did not have a firm alibi for his whereabouts on either the night of the kidnaping or the night the ransom was paid. His wife couldn't remember where he was on these nights when first questioned by the police, but suddenly did remember

Souvenir hunters in Flemington, New Jersey, with miniature "kidnap ladders" they bought from a local merchant. The name of the town is painted on the ladders. UPI/Corbis-Bettman.

when she testified during the trial. Reporters covering the proceedings had doubts about her testimony—and so, probably, did the jurors.

The state's case was by no means open-and-shut, however. The most glaring hole in it was Prosecutor Wilentz's inability to present a convincing outline of how the crime was committed.

In his opening statement to the jury, Wilentz speculated that Hauptmann had put the sleeping or drugged child in a sack. Then he had backed down the ladder from the nursery window with the sack clutched under one arm. But a rung in the ladder cracked—the sound

Charles had heard in the living room—and Hauptmann lost his grip on the sack. The baby fell headfirst to the paving stones below and died instantly from a fractured skull.

At first hearing this outline seemed plausible, but it left unanswered an important question. What if the rung hadn't cracked and Hauptmann and the baby had both reached the ground safely? Where did he intend to take the child? How did he plan to care for it?

In most instances it takes two or more people to bring off a kidnaping. One of them guards the victim while the other negotiates the ransom. A number of observers of the Hauptmann trial doubted that he could have carried out a plan as daring as the kidnaping of Charles Lindbergh Jr. all by himself. But Hauptmann never gave any indication that he had an accomplice—to do so would have meant admitting his own guilt. And no accomplice ever surfaced.

On the morning of February 13, 1935, more than six weeks after the trial began, the case finally went to the jury. All through the day and into the evening the jurors weighed the evidence while a crowd assembled outside the courthouse. As the hours passed without a verdict, those waiting in the courthouse square became impatient, then angry. Some of them began to chant, "Kill Hauptmann! Kill Hauptmann!"

Charles had left the courtroom when the case went to the jury and had returned to Englewood to await the verdict with Anne and her mother. Earlier, the Lindberghs had moved back to the Morrow mansion. That evening they were sitting in the living room after dinner, listening to the radio. Suddenly at ten forty-five the music program was interrupted and an announcer came on to report, "Bruno Hauptmann has been condemned to death without mercy!"

In the background could be heard the mob chanting outside the courthouse in Flemington. "That's a lynching mob," said Charles.

He and Anne went into the kitchen for ginger ale together with Mrs. Morrow and Harold Nicolson, a guest at the mansion. Nicolson was a well-known British author and diplomat. He had agreed to write a biography of Anne's father, Dwight Morrow, and was doing research for the book in Englewood.

Bruno Hauptmann, at left, confers with his lawyer, Edward J. Reilly, during a break in the trial. UPI/Corbis-Bettman.

"I don't know if you have followed this case very carefully," Charles said to Nicolson. "There is no doubt in my mind that Hauptmann did this thing. I am sure about this—quite sure. It is this way. . . ."

Then Charles proceeded to go through the entire case, point by point. He spoke very quietly, very simply. Although he seemed to be doing it for Nicolson's benefit, the Englishman could see that he was really trying to ease the tension his wife and mother-in-law were experiencing. Perhaps he was also trying to convince himself that Hauptmann was not only guilty but also the sole perpetrator of the crime.

Back in the courtroom, Prosecutor Wilentz asked for an immediate sentence. The judge agreed, and sentenced Hauptmann to death in the electric chair. That wasn't the end of the case, however. Hauptmann's attorneys filed appeals, postponing the execution. Meanwhile, his wife, Anna, toured the country speaking before German-American groups to raise money for her husband's court costs. In her speeches Anna Hauptmann claimed that Bruno had been framed by the police, that they had planted every item of the evidence used against him.

The Lindberghs tried to put the trial behind them and get on with their lives. Anne finished the manuscript of *North to the Orient*, and the book was published to glowing reviews in the late summer of 1935. Charles continued his scientific work at the Rockefeller Institute with his usual determination. At last, after four years of experiments, he and Dr. Alexis Carrel reported that they had succeeded in keeping a cat's thyroid gland alive in a perfusion pump for 120 days. The press called their accomplishment a major medical breakthrough.

No matter what they did, though, neither Charles nor Anne could escape the aftershocks of the trial for long. In October 1935 it made the headlines again when the New Jersey Court of Appeals denied Hauptmann's petition for a reversal of the verdict.

With the case back in the news, some of the more sensational New York newspapers decided to try to get candid photos of the Lindberghs' second son, Jon. The three-year-old was attending a nursery school in

Englewood. One afternoon a press car filled with photographers was waiting when Mrs. Morrow's chauffeur arrived to pick up Jon after school.

The photographers followed the boy's limousine and forced the vehicle to the side of the road. They jumped out of the press car, flashbulbs popping, and photographed the terrified Jon from every angle. He was still sobbing when the limousine sped away.

Charles became enraged when he heard about the incident. First Charles Jr. had been kidnaped and murdered. Now Jon had been frightened by photographers on his way home from school. What would happen next? Abruptly, Charles decided the only thing he and Anne could do to protect their son was to leave the country. "I'm taking my family to England," he confided to a *New York Times* reporter whom he trusted.

Lindbergh had become deeply disillusioned with his native land. "Our moral standards are low," he told the reporter. "It shows in the newspapers, the morbid curiosity over crimes and murder trials. Americans seem to have little respect for law, or the rights of others."

His tone became more personal. "I've got to get Anne and the baby away. There have been threats against the family. I'm going to make England my home." Why England? the reporter asked. Because, Charles replied, "I believe the English have a greater regard for law and order than the people of any other nation."

Back home in Englewood, in early December, he spoke quietly to Anne. "Be ready to go by the end of the week—at twenty-four hours' notice," he said.

✧ CHAPTER NINETEEN ✧

Hero in Exile

Charles booked passage on a small freighter bound for the British port of Liverpool. He and Anne and Jon were the only passengers on board, and they departed in complete secrecy. Not until the ship was far out at sea did *The New York Times* publish the exclusive story Charles had given its reporter.

"Although the Lindberghs do not plan to give up their American citizenship, they are prepared to live abroad permanently, if that should prove necessary," the article stated. It concluded: "And so the man who eight years ago was hailed as an international hero and a goodwill ambassador between the peoples of the world is taking his wife and son to establish, if he can, a secure haven for them in a foreign land."

In Englewood friends of Anne's mother said that "the entire family has been fearful for Jon's safety for months." The friends expressed relief along with "bitter regret" that the Lindberghs had left.

The president of the National Congress of Parents and Teachers said it was "unbelievable that conditions should make it impossible for people as valuable as the Lindberghs to live here." From one end of the country to the other, newspapers printed editorials blaming America for, as one put it, "driving from her shores her most famous citizen."

The *New York Daily News* was one of the few papers that thought Lindbergh himself was at least partly to blame for his problems. "He

Charles and Anne Lindbergh and their second son, Jon, are photographed through the window of their car as it speeds away from the dock in Liverpool, England. UPI/Corbis-Bettman.

would have been pestered less," the *News* said in an editorial, "if he had acted more as a popular hero is supposed to act, and been less embarrassed in the public gaze."

There was no question that the public was still fascinated by the Lindberghs. When the freighter carrying them docked in Liverpool on December 31, they were greeted by a huge gathering of reporters and photographers. The family hurried down the gangplank and into a waiting car that took them to their hotel. For a few days they were besieged in their suite by eager reporters. But after this flurry of interest, they were allowed to settle quietly into their new life.

In March 1936 the Lindberghs rented Long Barn, a sprawling old house in the English countryside near the village of Weald. Their landlords were Harold Nicolson and his novelist wife, Vita Sackville-West. In the meantime, back in New Jersey, the state's Court of Pardons denied Bruno Hauptmann's final appeal for clemency. On the evening of April 3—almost four years to the day after Dr. Condon handed over the $50,000 ransom to Graveyard John—Hauptmann was led into the execution chamber of the state penitentiary. He died in the electric chair, still protesting his innocence.

The Lindberghs made no public comment on Hauptmann's execution. Charles was busy working in the laboratory he had set up in one wing of Long Barn. Anne had a new writing project—*Listen! The Wind*, a book-length account of the Lindberghs' flights around the Atlantic in 1933.

In the late spring of 1936 Charles received an unexpected request from Truman Smith, the military attaché at the U.S. embassy in Berlin, Germany. It seemed that Hermann Göring, head of all aviation activities in Germany, had invited Charles to pay a visit to his country and see firsthand the progress Germany was making in aviation.

Smith urged Charles to accept Göring's invitation. Following its defeat in World War I, Germany had been disarmed. But after Adolf Hitler and his Nazi Party came to power in 1933, the country had begun a steady military buildup. U.S. intelligence forces weren't sure just how far that buildup had gone. An inspection tour by Charles could provide them with a more reliable estimate of German air strength.

With this in mind Charles agreed to go, and Anne decided to accompany him. Leaving Jon in the care of a nanny, they flew a rented plane to Berlin. They landed in the midst of preparations for the Olympic Games, which were being held in the German capital that summer. Anne noted the flags hanging everywhere—red Nazi flags with black swastikas on them and white Olympic flags with five interlocking circles.

The Nazis had arranged a full official schedule for the Lindberghs. Charles and Anne sat in General Göring's box at the opening-day ceremonies of the Olympics and received an ovation from the vast crowd.

Top: *Hermann Göring shows the Lindberghs around his luxurious office at the Air Ministry in Berlin during their 1936 visit to Germany. Note portrait of Adolf Hitler on Göring's desk.* Bottom: *Charles examines a German ceremonial sword in Göring's office.* Both photos from the Library of Congress.

Göring invited them to his palatial office at the Air Ministry, where he showed Charles photographs of Germany's military flying fields, each of them equipped with the most modern equipment. He also cleared the way for Charles to tour the country's main center of aeronautical research and the Heinkel and Junkers aircraft factories.

Charles was especially impressed by the powerful new Stuka dive-bomber that he saw on the assembly line at the Junkers plant. At the same time he realized the terrible destructive potential of these planes and other bombers like them. In a speech to an audience of German officers at the Berlin Air Club, he said: "We who are in aviation carry a heavy burden on our shoulders, for . . . aviation has, I believe, created the most fundamental change ever made in war. . . . We can no longer protect our families with an army. Our libraries, our museums, every institution we value most, are laid bare to bombardment."

But his dread of a future war fought in the air did not keep Charles from admiring Germany and the Germans. He knew that they were doing more than the people of any other country to prepare for just such an air war. Still, he couldn't help but respect their energy, efficiency, and sense of purpose.

Anne shared Charles's feelings. In a letter to her mother, she wrote that ". . . there is no question of the power, unity, and purposefulness of Germany. . . . It is thrilling when seen manifested in the energy, pride, and morale of the people—especially the young people."

There were things she, and presumably Charles, disliked about Nazi Germany: the persecution of the Jews, the regimentation of the German people. She also had some doubts about Adolf Hitler's one-man rule. But on balance she thought Hitler was "like an inspired religious leader—a visionary who really wants the best for his country."

In hindsight one may well wonder how Anne and Charles Lindbergh could have been so blind to the evil nature of Nazi Germany. They were by no means alone, however. The Great Depression, which had been going on for seven years, had shattered the faith of many Americans in capitalism and the democratic system of government that embraced it.

Some Americans looked to communism, as it was being developed in the Soviet Union, for answers to capitalism's problems. In so doing, they ignored the crimes the Soviet leader, Joseph Stalin, was committing against his own people. Other Americans, like the Lindberghs, found the fascist policies of Nazi Germany more acceptable than communism. They, in turn, ignored or tried to minimize Adolf Hitler's crimes against the German people.

Upon his return to England, Charles met with high government officials and reported on the advances Germany was making in aviation. He tried to convince the officials of the need to build up Britain's air force rapidly as a counter to the German threat. The officials listened politely but took no immediate action, leaving Charles to wonder why he had bothered.

In the spring of 1937 Anne gave birth in London to the Lindberghs' third son. They named him Land, after Charles's Grandfather Land. That fall Charles accepted a second invitation to visit Germany, and once again Anne accompanied him. They flew first to Frankfurt and then to Munich, where Charles was to attend an aviation congress.

At the congress Charles made friends with Ernst Udet, the World War I German air ace whose exploits had thrilled the teenage Lindbergh. Now a high official in the Air Ministry, Udet obtained permission for Charles to visit a top-secret military airfield after the congress was over. There Charles inspected seven of the latest German warplanes and got to test fly a new bomber.

Before leaving Germany, Charles wrote a lengthy memorandum for the U.S. military attaché describing what he had seen and heard on the trip. Throughout, the report emphasized the strengths of the German air force, the Luftwaffe. It omitted any mention of the Luftwaffe's weaknesses, which included a lack of long-range bombers and the inexperience of many German officers. This made veteran reporters in Berlin like William L. Shirer wonder whom Charles was serving more effectively: U.S. intelligence or Hitler's propaganda machine?

Whatever its shortcomings, Charles's memorandum obviously impressed the higher-ups in Washington. They asked Charles to return to the United States and brief the National Council for Aeronautics in

Top: *Charles on an inspection tour of a German military airfield during his 1937 trip.* Bottom: *His German hosts arranged for Charles to test fly a new warplane.* Both photos from the Missouri Historical Society, St. Louis.

person. Leaving Jon and baby Land with their nannies, he and Anne sailed home to America in December 1937, just two years after they had fled their country's shores.

The Lindberghs remained in the States for three months, staying at the Morrow mansion in Englewood, seeing family and friends, and managing to avoid publicity. They returned to England in March 1938, just as Hitler's storm troops marched into neighboring Austria and made it part of Germany. Britain and France were upset by this new example of Hitler's aggression, but they took no action against it.

In May the Lindberghs left England and moved to an old stone house on Illiec, a tiny island off the northeast coast of France. Both Charles and Anne had become disenchanted with England, where they had made few friends, and welcomed the idea of a change. So when the opportunity to buy Illiec came along, they leaped at it.

The island's former owner was Charles's old friend Dr. Alexis Carrel, who spent his summers on a larger island nearby. The Lindberghs' new home on Illiec contained nine rooms, but it had no electricity or running water. Charles loved the remoteness of the island, though. He told Anne he hadn't enjoyed living in a place so much since his boyhood years in Little Falls.

While the Lindberghs were getting settled on their rocky island, Hitler began to put pressure on another of Germany's neighbors, Czechoslovakia. He charged that the Czechs were persecuting the German-speaking people who lived in the region of Czechoslovakia known as the Sudetenland. This time Britain and France took a firmer stand than they had with Austria. They warned Hitler that he risked a wider conflict if he moved against Czechoslovakia.

As tension mounted in Central Europe that summer, the American military attaché in London asked Charles to visit the Soviet Union and tour its aviation facilities. U.S. intelligence agencies had found his estimates of German air strength extremely useful. Now they wanted him to make a similar appraisal of air strength in the Soviet Union—another potential threat to world peace.

✦ CHAPTER TWENTY ✦

A German Medal

Charles felt it his duty to go to the Soviet Union, and in August he and Anne flew to Moscow in their new British-built plane. They were warmly greeted at the airport by authorities from the U.S. embassy and key officials of Soviet civil aviation.

Although the Soviet capital seemed more prosperous than it had in 1933, when the Lindberghs were there previously, Charles was not impressed by what he saw of Soviet aviation. The country's planes appeared to be inferior copies of European and American models, and the machinery in many aircraft factories was worn and out-of-date.

He and Anne were entertained lavishly by their Soviet hosts but found them reluctant to talk freely. In 1938 the Soviet leader, Joseph Stalin, was busily purging the Soviet government and military of persons suspected of being "enemies of the state." An offhand remark could cost a person his job or even his life if overheard by one of Stalin's secret agents. Consequently, the Lindberghs' hosts were extremely careful about what they said in casual conversation.

Charles and Anne both noted this tension. "Russian life is as close to hell on earth as it is possible for human beings to come," Charles wrote later to a cousin in the States. It's curious that he never seemed to notice a similar atmosphere of repression in Nazi Germany.

The Lindberghs flew back to France via Czechoslovakia, which

Germany continued to threaten. Charles admired the Czech military officials he met, but he didn't think the country's air force would be any match for the Luftwaffe if Germany attacked. Czech planes lacked speed and power, and there weren't enough of them.

When the Lindberghs returned to Paris, they found the French capital filled with gloom. Many people feared that war would break out any day over Czechoslovakia. Hitler's demand that Germany be given the Sudetenland had grown louder and more insistent over the summer. At the same time, the Czech government was trying to get firm commitments of support from the two nations with whom it had treaties of mutual assistance, France and the Soviet Union.

The Soviet Union said it would come to the Czechs' aid in case of a German attack, provided France did also. The French wavered. They were reluctant to enter into any sort of alliance with the communist government of the Soviet Union. Instead, they looked to Great Britain to join them in defending Czechoslovakia, even if it meant going to war against Germany.

The British government, like the French, was of two minds about the matter. Those in favor of helping the Czechs were almost evenly balanced with those who thought the wiser course of action would be to give Hitler what he wanted and avoid a devastating war.

As the Czech crisis mounted toward a climax, and Britain and France tried to decide whether or not to intervene, air power emerged as the crucial factor. What were the relative air strengths of Germany, France, England, and the Soviet Union? No one seemed better equipped to answer that question than Charles Lindbergh.

In Paris Charles met with the French minister for air, Guy la Chambre, who told him that French factories were producing only forty-five to fifty warplanes a month, and England about seventy. La Chambre estimated that Germany, on the other hand, was turning out between five hundred and eight hundred planes monthly, and asked Charles if he thought that estimate was correct.

Yes, Charles said, and added that, in his opinion, the German air force was stronger than those of all the Western European countries combined. As for the Soviet air force, he judged it inferior in every way to Germany's.

Two weeks after his meeting with la Chambre, Charles was summoned to London by the U.S. ambassador to Great Britain, Joseph P. Kennedy. Kennedy (the father of future president John F. Kennedy) was a staunch isolationist. That meant he believed the United States should do everything possible to isolate itself from European conflicts and avoid becoming entangled in a new world war.

Kennedy knew that the governments of Britain and France were debating whether or not to go to war with Germany over Czechoslovakia. He hoped Charles could give him concrete information about German air strength. With that in hand, Kennedy thought, he could convince President Roosevelt to put pressure on the leaders of Britain and France to come to terms with Hitler. Otherwise, Kennedy believed, the European democracies would find themselves involved in an air war they couldn't possibly win. And America might be dragged into it.

Charles gave Kennedy the same estimate of German air strength that he had given la Chambre. The ambassador asked him to put it in writing, and Charles did so at once. The next day his report was cabled in code to Washington.

While he was in London, Charles also talked with Group Captain John Slessor, deputy director of the British Air Ministry. Some time later Slessor wrote his impressions of Lindbergh. He called Charles "an extremely likable person, transparently honest and sincere." But, Slessor concluded, "His very decency and naïveté led me, in submitting my report of our conversation, to express the view that . . . he was also a striking example of the effect of German propaganda."

Slessor's impression of Lindbergh may have been accurate. But Britain's leaders took Charles seriously, and his estimates of German air power helped them decide to appease Hitler rather than confront him. On September 29, 1938, British Prime Minister Neville Chamberlain flew to Munich, Germany, for a conference with Hitler. French Premier Édouard Daladier joined them there. Together Chamberlain and Daladier agreed to let Hitler strip the Sudetenland away from Czechoslovakia and make it a part of Germany.

Huge crowds greeted Chamberlain and Daladier when they returned home to their respective capitals. In an airport speech Chamberlain said he had brought back from Germany "peace with honor." Acknowledging the crowd's cheers, he added, "I believe it is peace in our time."

British Prime Minister Neville Chamberlain proclaims "Peace in our time" upon his return from Munich, where he met with Adolf Hitler. Corbis-Bettman.

Ten days later Charles and Anne Lindbergh flew to Berlin, where Charles was to take part in another aviation conference. He and Anne also wanted to look into the possibility of spending the winter months in Berlin with Jon and Land. Their stone house on Illiec was not habitable in cold weather. Besides, Charles thought it would be stimulating to live for a time in Germany, which he considered to be the world leader in aviation at the moment. Germany was also the only country, except for the Soviet Union, where the press never hounded him or his family. Somehow Charles managed to overlook the fact that this was because the German press was strictly controlled by its Nazi overlords.

On the evening of October 19 Charles was the guest of honor at a stag dinner in Berlin. The American ambassador to Germany, Hugh R. Wilson, hosted the affair, which was attended by high Nazi officials. General Hermann Göring was the last to arrive. He strode over to Charles and announced that he was there "by order of the führer, Adolf Hitler," to present Charles with the Service Cross of the German Eagle and its accompanying star.

This award, the second highest of all German decorations, had been created to honor distinguished foreigners who had served Germany in some significant way. The official announcement said it had been given to Charles for his contributions to world aviation. But there were those who wondered if it was really meant to reward him for his help in bringing about the Munich Agreement of Hitler, Chamberlain, and Daladier.

Whatever the reason for the award, Charles stood patiently in the embassy dining room while Göring hung around his neck the Service Cross suspended from a ribbon, and pinned on his chest the six-pointed silver star. A *New York Times* reporter who was present wrote that "Colonel Lindbergh appeared surprised and displayed an embarrassed smile, but thanked General Göring . . . and proudly wore the decoration throughout the evening."

Anne Lindbergh had a very different reaction when Charles came home and showed her the cross and star. She took one look at the award and called it "the albatross." That expression signaled Anne's fear that the Nazi prize would be a troublesome burden for her husband.

Charles dismissed Anne's worries at the time, but future events would prove her right. Reactions to the award in Great Britain, France, and the United States were a mixture of shocked surprise and anger. Speaking in Cleveland, U.S. Secretary of the Interior Harold L. Ickes asked: "How can any American accept a decoration at the hand of a brutal dictator who, with that same hand, is robbing and torturing thousands of fellow human beings?"

A German woman laughs as she passes a Jewish-owned store wrecked on Kristallnacht, *November 9, 1938.* UPI/Corbis-Bettman.

Charles ignored the criticisms and returned to France with Anne. But he continued to have his agents in Berlin search for a suitable house for the family to rent that winter. Then, on the night of November 9, the Nazis launched a surprise attack on Jewish businesses and synagogues throughout Germany and Austria. So many store windows were broken during the assault that it became known as *Kristallnacht*, the "night of broken glass." More than a hundred Jews were killed on *Kristallnacht*, and thousands of others were arrested when they tried to defend their shops.

People throughout the world were stunned by this latest example of Nazi ruthlessness. President Franklin D. Roosevelt expressed the feelings of millions of Americans when he said, "The news of the past few days from Germany has deeply shocked public opinion in the United States. . . . I myself can scarcely believe that such things could occur in a twentieth-century civilization."

Charles made no public comment on *Kristallnacht*. But he phoned his representatives in Berlin to say that, under the circumstances, he was no longer thinking of spending the winter in Germany. Instead, he and Anne rented an apartment in Paris for themselves and their two boys.

In the spring of 1939 General Henry H. (Hap) Arnold, chief of the U.S. Army Air Corps, asked Charles to come back to America. Charles was still a colonel in the U.S. Air Corps Reserve, and General Arnold needed his advice on how best to reinforce America's air strength. Fears of war in Europe were rising once more, and Arnold wanted the United States to be prepared for whatever might happen.

Charles was reluctant to leave Europe but could not disobey the order of his commanding officer. On April 14 he set sail for America by himself on the liner *Aquitania*. Anne and the children would follow later on another ship in an attempt to avoid publicity. Whether the Lindberghs liked it or not, their comings and goings were still news.

CHAPTER TWENTY-ONE

Speaking Out

Four days after his return, Colonel Charles Lindbergh reported for active duty in Washington. He was immediately thrust into a round of meetings with War Department officers and the heads of civilian research agencies. Out of the meetings came recommendations for a huge buildup of the Army Air Corps. Congress appropriated millions of dollars for the buildup, and the Air Corps set a goal of 6,000 new warplanes.

That spring and summer Charles toured the United States, inspecting aircraft research and manufacturing facilities from coast to coast. Meanwhile, Anne and the boys settled into a rented house on the north shore of Long Island. Charles joined them on weekends and enjoyed walking on the beach with Anne and swimming in Long Island Sound with his two sons.

Although Charles saw the need for the United States to strengthen its defenses, he hadn't changed his opinion about the military situation in Europe. He still believed that Britain and France were weak and that Nazi Germany could not be beaten on the ground or in the air. In line with this, he felt strongly that the United States should do everything in its power to stay out of any war that started in Europe. He was by no means alone; many Americans supported this isolationist position.

One evening in July Charles met the conservative radio commentator

Fulton Lewis Jr. at a dinner in Washington. Charles freely expressed his views on the European scene, and Lewis liked what he heard. "The American people ought to know how you feel about things," he said. He offered to help arrange for Charles to make a nationwide radio broadcast.

Charles was pleased with the idea but said there was no way he could give such a talk while on active duty in the Air Corps. He added, though, that he'd take a rain check on the offer.

In the meantime tensions in Europe were mounting rapidly. The Munich Agreement had not satisfied Hitler's desire for more territory. In March 1939 Germany had taken over the rest of Czechoslovakia. Two weeks later Hitler's ally Benito Mussolini, the fascist leader of Italy, occupied the tiny country of Albania. This gave Mussolini the springboard for a future attack on Greece. At the same time, Germany began to put pressure on Poland, its neighbor to the east.

Alarmed by these moves, Britain and France offered what they called "security guarantees" to Greece, Poland, and Romania. All these countries were now menaced by Germany or Italy, or both. The three countries immediately accepted the guarantees. But their leaders wondered privately how Britain and France would be able to enforce them.

Joseph Stalin, leader of the Soviet Union, wondered too. In the wake of the Munich Agreement he became convinced that the Western democracies Britain and France could not be trusted. If Hitler decided to move against the Soviet Union, Stalin was quite sure neither Britain nor France would come to his country's aid.

And so, in August 1939—while Charles Lindbergh was swimming in Long Island Sound with his sons—Joseph Stalin stunned the world by signing a nonaggression pact with Hitler. At the heart of the pact was a promise that the Soviet Union and Germany would not attack each other. The pact bought Stalin time to build up the Soviet Union's defenses, since he didn't trust Hitler any more than he trusted the leaders of Britain and France. It also freed Germany to attack Poland without fear that the Soviet Union would raise any objection.

Polish young people look up in fear and anger as German planes drop bombs on their capital city, Warsaw, in September 1939. UPI/Corbis-Bettman.

That is exactly what happened. On September 1, 1939, less than ten days after the pact was signed, Germany invaded Poland. A day later Great Britain and France declared war on Hitler's Germany. According to the security guarantees both countries had signed with Poland, there was nothing else they could do. World War II, which so many people had feared for so many years, had begun.

Three days after the declaration of war, Charles phoned Fulton Lewis Jr. "I want to talk to you about the radio broadcast you suggested," Charles said.

Lindbergh had requested a release from active duty, and the request was granted on September 14. Now he was free to say whatever he wanted in the radio talk. But he was still an active member of an important Air Corps committee. When word got out that he planned to broadcast his thoughts on the war in Europe, some army officers tried to get him to cancel the talk.

President Roosevelt was behind this effort. He hadn't forgotten the role Lindbergh had played in the airmail controversy of 1934, and how strongly the public had supported the airman's stand. Now Roosevelt worried that the public would respond just as favorably to Lindbergh's isolationist views on the war.

The president knew a majority of the American people were opposed to U.S. involvement, and he had no desire to lead the nation into battle. Especially not with a presidential election coming up in 1940. At the same time, Roosevelt saw the war as a life-and-death struggle between the forces of democracy, represented by Great Britain and France, and the forces of fascism, embodied in Hitler's Germany and Mussolini's Italy. He did not think the United States could simply stand by and allow the democracies to lose.

Roosevelt appreciated Lindbergh's expertise in aviation even as he disagreed with the pilot's political views. Perhaps Charles could be tempted into silence by the offer of a high government post—say the command of a separate air force on a par with the Army and the Navy.

A few days before the radio broadcast was to take place, a representative of the president suggested this possibility to Charles. He flatly rejected the idea, seeing it as a kind of bribe. If Roosevelt had hoped the offer would make Charles think twice about speaking out, it had the exact opposite effect. Charles was now more determined than ever to go forward with the broadcast.

He spoke from a studio in Washington over all three major radio networks on the evening of September 15, 1939. Millions of Americans tuned in, eager to hear the hero-pilot of 1927 who had been in the news ever since, yet had rarely spoken in public. They heard him say, in a clear, unemotional voice, "I speak tonight to those Americans who feel that the destiny of this country does not call for our involvement in European wars."

Reading word for word from a text he had written himself, Charles

Charles Lindbergh broadcasts over all three major radio networks on September 15, 1939, urging that the United States stay out of the war in Europe. UPI/Corbis-Bettman.

went on: "These wars in Europe are not wars in which our civilization is defending itself against some Asiatic intruder. . . . This is not a question of banding together to defend the white race against foreign invasion. This is simply one more of those age-old struggles within our family of nations."

The speech drew a huge amount of mail from listeners and evoked a wide range of responses pro and con. Spokesmen of the Roosevelt administration criticized Charles's "presumption" in "posing as an expert in foreign policy." Liberal commentators reminded their readers of Lindbergh's German medal and charged that he had helped bring about the appeasement of Hitler at Munich. Many were shocked by the racist views expressed in the speech.

But Charles had numerous supporters, too. From the right end of the political spectrum came those who held isolationist views, confirmed Roosevelt haters, and backers of Nazi Germany. Joining them from the left were Christian pacifists who opposed any and all wars and members of the American Communist Party. The Communists had adopted an isolationist position after the Soviet Union signed its nonaggression pact with Germany.

Besides these groups, there were also the millions of Americans who remembered Charles's Paris flight and still hero-worshiped "Lucky Lindy."

Encouraged by the many letters and phone calls from his supporters, Charles made plans for another speech to be delivered a month later, on October 13. By then Poland had been totally defeated—the western sector occupied by the Nazis, the eastern by the Russians. This arrangement was a secret part of the Nazi-Soviet nonaggression pact.

In his second talk Charles focused on the embargo of arms sales to other countries that was being debated in Congress. He didn't believe lifting the embargo would assist the forces of democracy in Europe, he said, because he didn't think this was a struggle for democracy. In his opinion, "This is a war over the balance of power in Europe—a war brought about by the desire for strength on the part of Germany and the fear of that strength on the part of England and France."

Once again he sounded a racist note. "Our bond with Europe is a bond of race and not of political ideology. . . . If the white race is ever seriously threatened, it may then be time for us to take our part for its protection, to fight side by side with the English, French, and Germans. But not with one against the other for our mutual destruction."

As controversy swirled around him, Charles in December resigned from the National Advisory Committee for Aeronautics, the last government committee he was serving on. After that he expressed his views even more forcefully. In an article published in *Atlantic Monthly* in March 1940, he wrote that the conflict in Europe was not between right and wrong, as many Americans believed. Rather, he said, it was between "two differing concepts of right." For Lindbergh there was apparently no moral difference between the actions of the Western democracies and those of Hitler's Germany.

Until then the Western front in Europe had remained quiet. Ever since the fall of Poland, the German and French armies had been entrenched opposite each other in massive fortifications along their respective borders. Four divisions of British soldiers were stationed in northern France to help defend their ally in case the Germans attacked France through Belgium.

All that changed in April 1940. With lightning speed the German army occupied Denmark, then went on to invade and conquer Norway. In May the Nazis swept across the Netherlands, Luxembourg, and Belgium, and broke through the French defenses with an unbeatable combination of tanks on the ground and warplanes in the air. Within just three weeks they had soundly defeated the once-proud French army and forced its British supporters to retreat to England in a patchwork fleet of small boats.

Now Britain stood alone against the mighty German army and air force. Day and night Hitler's planes pounded the city of London and other British targets in one bombing raid after another. These fierce attacks soon became known as "the Blitz," after the German word for lightning.

To many Americans, including Charles Lindbergh, the fight for free-

A building hit by German bombs topples into a London street during the Blitz of 1940. In the background can be seen the dome of St. Paul's Cathedral. Library of Congress.

dom in Europe seemed close to hopeless. In June 1940 he said in another radio talk, "We must face the fact, regardless of how disagreeable it is to us, that before we can take effective action in a European war, the German armies may have brought all Europe under their control."

But most Americans still hoped the outcome would be different. They might not want the United States to enter the war itself, and commit young Americans to the conflict, but they were willing to support Britain in every way short of war. That led the Republican Party in the summer of 1940 to pass over a number of conservative candidates for president and nominate a moderate businessman, Wendell Willkie. Willkie disagreed with President Roosevelt's domestic policies, but he endorsed Roosevelt's pro-British foreign policy.

Not Charles Lindbergh. In August 1940, while British cities were being battered by German bombers, he made a speech in Chicago. "In the past we have dealt with a Europe dominated by England and France," he said. "In the future we may have to deal with a Europe dominated by Germany. . . ."

After this speech even some of those who had been willing to give Charles the benefit of the doubt began to think of him as pro-Nazi. The historian James Truslow Adams said it was "evident that Lindbergh's sympathies are with Germany and that he is strongly biased against England." A well-known foreign correspondent, H. R. Knickerbocker, was even more critical of Charles. He wrote: "His policy shamelessly declares we should withdraw aid from Britain, coolly watch her fall, and then as quickly as possible trade with Hitler and make what we can out of the defeat of civilization."

In the fall of 1940 Anne Lindbergh gave birth to a daughter. Charles was insistent that the baby be named Anne, after her mother. That fall Mrs. Lindbergh also published a new book, titled *The Wave of the Future*. In it she echoed many of Charles's views on the struggle in Europe between the forces of democracy and the forces of fascism.

Because of the public's continuing fascination with the Lindberghs, *The Wave of the Future* quickly became a best-seller. But many critics accused it of being profascist. One of them was E. B. White, author of *Charlotte's Web* and *Stuart Little*, as well as books and articles for adults. In an essay published in *The New Yorker* he wrote, "Mrs. Lindbergh says: 'I do feel that it is futile to get into a hopeless "crusade" to save civilization.' Maybe it is, but I do not think it entirely futile to take up arms to dispossess tyrants, defend popular government, and promote free methods."

Critical remarks like White's upset Anne. No amount of negative comments could shake Charles's confidence, however. He was convinced the stand he had taken against the war was in the best interests of the United States.

Lindbergh testifies against the Lend-Lease Bill before the Senate Foreign Relations Committee in February 1941. UPI/Corbis-Bettman.

In February 1941 Congress was debating the Lend-Lease Bill, which the Roosevelt administration had proposed. The bill would give the president the authority to sell, lend, or lease war supplies to nations such as Great Britain whose survival was considered vital to the defense of the United States.

Charles testified against the bill in both the Senate and the House of Representatives. Speaking before the Senate's Foreign Relations Committee, he expressed doubts that American aid to Great Britain would do any good. "Personally, I do not believe that England is in a position to win the war," he said.

When he appeared before the Foreign Relations Committee of the House, a representative from Tennessee asked him bluntly, "Whom do you *want* to win this war?" Charles looked coldly at the man and said, "I want neither side to win." He favored a negotiated peace, he said. Apparently it did not disturb him that Adolf Hitler would dictate the terms . . . just as he had at Munich.

But Great Britain, under the leadership of a new prime minister, Winston Churchill, was not about to enter into any sort of negotiated peace with its archenemy, Hitler. Britain had not only survived the Blitz but had shot down so many German planes that Hitler had been forced to delay his plans to invade the island empire. British morale got another boost in March, when Congress passed the Lend-Lease Bill, despite the objections of Charles and other isolationists.

This defeat did not sway Charles from the course he had chosen. Quite the contrary, in fact. Until then he had operated entirely on his own. Now, in April 1941, he joined an isolationist organization known as America First and accepted a post on its executive committee.

Many other prominent Americans were members of America First. These included General Robert E. Ward, chairman of the board of Sears, Roebuck; actress Lillian Gish; World War I air ace Eddie Rickenbacker; and auto manufacturer Henry Ford. But the undoubted star of America First was Charles Lindbergh, who could fill a huge auditorium whenever he spoke.

✧ CHAPTER TWENTY-TWO ✧

America First

On April 17, 1941, Charles addressed a cheering crowd at an America First rally in Chicago. A week later, with Anne sitting on the platform beside him, he spoke to an even more enthusiastic gathering in New York's vast Madison Square Garden. Ignoring Great Britain's recent victories, he predicted that the country would soon go down to defeat, and said no amount of U.S. aid could prevent it.

By the spring of 1941 polls showed that 60 percent of the American people believed it was more important for the United States to help Britain win the war than to stay out of it. But Charles Lindbergh still had a strong influence over the remaining 40 percent. As a result the Roosevelt administration could not provide Britain with as much aid as it wanted to.

At a press conference reporters asked President Roosevelt what he thought of Charles's isolationist speeches. In reply the president said there had always been naysayers like Lindbergh in times of national crisis. He compared Charles to Clement L. Vallandigham, an Ohio congressman during the Civil War. The congressman had made violent speeches against President Lincoln's policies, arguing that the North could never win its war against the South.

Charles was hurt and angry when he read Roosevelt's remarks. He brooded about them over a long weekend, then wrote the president a letter that he released at the same time to the press. In it he said: "I had hoped that I might exercise my right as an American citizen to place my viewpoint before the people of my country in time of peace without giving up the privilege of serving my country as an Air Corps officer in the event of war."

But, he went on, "in view of implications that you, my President and superior officer, have made concerning my loyalty to my country, my character, and my motives, I can see no alternative to tendering my resignation as colonel in the United States Air Corps reserve. . . ." He ended the letter by saying, "I will continue to serve my country to the best of my ability as a private citizen."

In the late spring and summer of 1941 that meant speaking at one America First rally after another. Meanwhile, the military situation in Europe took an unexpected turn. Unable to break England's spirit, Germany looked eastward instead. On June 22 Hitler shoved aside the nonaggression pact he had signed with the Soviet Union and launched an all-out attack on his former ally.

The democracies reacted swiftly. The United States extended its Lend-Lease policy to include the Soviet Union, and Great Britain promised all possible aid to the Soviets. But Lindbergh's outlook did not change. Speaking at a rally in San Francisco, he said: "I would a thousand times rather see my country ally herself with Germany than with Soviet Russia."

Supporters of America First applauded Charles's speeches enthusiastically. But many other Americans were appalled by them. Some urged that his name be removed from monuments put up in his honor after the Paris flight. In Chicago it was announced that the world's tallest airplane beacon would no longer be known as the Lindbergh Beacon. In Charlotte, North Carolina, the city council changed the name of Lindbergh Drive to Avon Avenue.

Even some of his relatives and closest friends turned against Charles. Harry Guggenheim, his early backer, no longer saw the Lindberghs

Top: *Charles Lindbergh addresses a sold-out America First rally at the Philadelphia Arena, May 29, 1941.* Bottom: *Women attending the Philadelphia rally applaud Anne Lindbergh.* Both photos from UPI/Corbis-Bettman.

socially. His mother-in-law, Betty Morrow, showed her displeasure with his isolationist stand by working hard to organize aid for Great Britain. His cousin Admiral Emory S. Land had no patience with Charles's views, either. "He's got into the wrong hands," the admiral said in an interview. "I just can't talk about him anymore. He's all wrong."

How could Charles go on in the face of such rejections? Perhaps he was sustained by the memory of his father, who had risked his political career to oppose America's entry into World War I. Certainly he was encouraged by the unwavering loyalty of his wife, Anne. Above all, the conviction that he was right enabled him to ignore all the criticisms and continue to speak his mind.

This stubborn determination of his had served Charles well when he was planning and carrying out his flight to Paris. But now, in very different circumstances, it was about to bring his reputation crashing down. On September 11, 1941, he was scheduled to speak at an America First rally in Des Moines, Iowa. As he sat at his desk writing the speech, he decided it was time to name names and let his audience know exactly which groups were pushing the United States toward war.

When he showed the talk to Anne, she was "thrust into black gloom," according to her diary. She got him to tone down some of the more questionable paragraphs but still experienced "a sinking of heart" as he left for Des Moines. She feared the effect of the speech—what it would start, and the impact it would have on Charles. As things turned out, her fears were more than justified.

Charles had often referred to different races in his speeches, but till now he had never made any antisemitic remarks. That changed with the Des Moines talk. In its most controversial passage, he stated flatly that "the three most important groups who have been pressing this country toward war are the Roosevelt administration, the British, and the Jews."

He went on to say he could understand why the Jews were so strongly opposed to Hitler. "The persecutions they suffered in Germany would be sufficient to make bitter enemies of any race." But, he said, "Instead of agitating for war the Jewish groups in this country should be opposing it in every possible way, for they will be among the first to feel its consequences. . . .

"A few far-sighted Jewish people realize this," he added. "But the majority still do not. Their greatest danger to this country lies in their large ownership and influence in our motion pictures, our press, our radio, and our government."

Those last sentences set off a firestorm of negative reactions. *The Des Moines Register* said in an editorial, "It may have been courageous for Colonel Lindbergh to say what was on his mind, but it was so lacking in appreciation of consequences that it disqualifies him for any pretensions of leadership in policy-making. . . ."

Even the conservative Hearst newspapers, which had been among Charles's strongest supporters, criticized him now. One of the papers commented: "Charles A. Lindbergh's intemperate and intolerant address in Des Moines, in which racial and religious prejudices were incited—especially against those of the Jewish faith—should arouse universal protest and denunciation."

Wendell Willkie, the Republican candidate for president the year before, called it "the most un-American talk made in my time by any person of a national reputation."

Anne felt many of the criticisms were unfair. Charles, she thought, had merely said in public what many of his critics said in private but were afraid to express openly. Charles himself did not seem to understand why he was being attacked. Speaking at another rally in Fort Wayne, Indiana, he made no apologies for anything in the Des Moines talk and said he had only been trying to tell the "truth" as he saw it.

Why had Charles adopted such a controversial position? What made him turn against Great Britain, make excuses for Nazi Germany, and now wade into the swamp of antisemitism? The British writer Harold Nicolson offered one of the best and clearest explanations for his behavior. Nicolson had observed Charles firsthand at the time of the Hauptmann trial, and later had been his landlord in Britain. Writing in a British magazine, Nicolson said:

*By the early fall of 1941 Lindbergh's America First speeches had become more fer-
vent—and more controversial.* UPI/Corbis-Bettman.

"After the Paris flight, it was almost with ferocity that he [Charles] struggled to remain himself. And in the process of that struggle his simplicity became muscle-bound, his self-control thickened into arrogance, and his convictions hardened into granite." In Nicolson's opinion, Charles had come to believe his own publicity, "the legend of the young lad from Minnesota whose head could not be turned."

Nicolson went on to speculate that the kidnaping and murder of his firstborn son had made Charles even more rigid. "He identified the outrage to his private life first with the popular press and then by inevitable associations with freedom of speech and, almost, with freedom itself. He began to loathe democracy." Once he had gone that far, Nicolson theorized, it was easy for Charles to reject Great Britain, accept Nazi Germany, and struggle fiercely to keep the United States out of the war.

That struggle would soon come to an abrupt end. By the late fall of 1941 Britain had won the battle for control of the North Atlantic sea-lanes and the Soviet army was proving to be a much stronger foe than Hitler had anticipated. Meanwhile, in Japan, the moderate premier, Prince Fumimaro Konoye, had been replaced by a military leader, General Hideki Tojo, who had close ties to Nazi Germany and fascist Italy. The threat of Japanese aggression in the Pacific grew. And then, on December 7, 1941, the Japanese mounted a surprise attack on the U.S. naval base at Pearl Harbor in the Hawaiian Islands.

Within minutes after news of the attack came through, reporters tried to see Charles at the house where he and his family were staying on Martha's Vineyard. He refused to meet with them. He also refused to answer any telephone calls or telegrams questioning him about his reactions to the attack and his future plans.

The next day, December 8, President Roosevelt went before a joint session of Congress and asked for a declaration of war on Japan. That day Charles issued a statement through the national headquarters of America First. In it he said, "We have been stepping closer to war for many months. Now it has come, and we must meet it as united Americans regardless of our attitude in the past toward the policy our government has followed." The executive committee of America First decided to cancel all future meetings and rallies.

Three days later, on December 11, Germany and Italy showed their support for Japan by declaring war on the United States also. The U.S. Congress responded in kind, with only one dissenting vote. It was cast by Jeannette Rankin of Montana, the first woman to be elected to Congress. Now America was at war on two fronts.

In his America First statement, Charles had said, "We must now turn every effort to building up the greatest and most efficient Army, Navy, and Air Force in the world." Late in December he signaled his desire to take part in that effort. He wrote a letter to his old friend, General Hap Arnold, volunteering his services in the Air Corps.

General Arnold wanted to accept Charles's offer. But higher-ups in the Roosevelt administration, among them the secretary of war and the president himself, were opposed to it. They hadn't forgotten his isolationist speeches, and they didn't believe he had changed his views. Charles Lindbergh, the great hero of 1927, had transformed himself into an object of suspicion—a man whose loyalty to his country could not be trusted.

CHAPTER TWENTY-THREE

"I Would Rather Have Birds Than Airplanes"

Charles Lindbergh would live for thirty-two more years and accomplish a great many things. He would never again play a major role in public life, though. And he would never completely regain his lost reputation.

After being rejected by the Air Corps at the start of the war, Charles sought employment with an aircraft manufacturer. But Pan American, Curtiss-Wright, and United Aircraft all turned him down. Word had come from Washington that the government would not look favorably on any company that hired Charles. Only Henry Ford, who had supported America First, was willing to ignore the War Department's warnings. He engaged Charles as a consultant on the production of the B-24 bomber.

Charles and Anne and their three children moved to Bloomfield Hills, a wealthy suburb of Detroit. There, in August 1942, Anne gave birth to the Lindberghs' fifth child, a boy whom they named Scott. Living in Michigan enabled Charles to see more of his mother, who was still teaching chemistry in a Detroit high school. The elder Mrs. Lindbergh took particular delight in being so close to her four lively grandchildren.

Besides working as a consultant at Ford, Charles upgraded his flying skills at a local airfield. He also volunteered to serve as a human guinea pig in tests of new oxygen equipment at high altitudes.

By 1944 the furor over Charles's America First activities had faded enough for him to be offered other aircraft consulting jobs. He accepted one with United Aircraft to help develop the F-4U Corvair fighter, which United was building for the Navy and the Marine Corps. Eager to see military action, Charles got himself approved as a civilian observer for United in the Pacific combat zone.

General Robert B. McClure shows Charles a late-model rifle during Lindbergh's visit to the Solomon Islands in the South Pacific, 1944. National Air and Space Museum, Smithsonian Institution.

He hitched rides across the Pacific on military planes until he reached the Solomon Islands. At air bases on the islands he studied the performance of the F-4U Corvair and advised their pilots on fuel efficiency. Charles also got the pilots to overlook regulations and let him accompany them on combat patrols over Japanese-held New Guinea. He strafed targets on the ground and got into a dogfight with a Japanese fighter.

The Japanese plane flew straight at him, guns ablaze, and Charles fired back. The two planes came within about ten feet of each other. Then the Japanese fighter swerved to one side, smoke streaming out of it, and crashed into the ocean.

When word got out that Charles was taking part in combat missions, he was immediately grounded. It was strictly forbidden for a civilian to fly military planes. But by then Charles had completed fifty missions and satisfied his desire to get a taste of the war. He returned to the States and continued to work as a consultant for United Aircraft in Connecticut until the end of the war in Europe in May 1945.

Later that month he flew to defeated Germany as a member of a team of aviation experts. Their task: to interview German aeronautical engineers and scientists and find out how far the Nazis had gotten in the development of rockets and jet aircraft. They also hoped to persuade the German experts to contribute their knowledge to the Western powers rather than the Soviet Union.

At Nordhausen in the mountains of central Germany, Lindbergh toured the notorious Camp Dora. This concentration camp had supplied slave labor to the huge V-2 rocket factory that the Nazis had built in underground tunnels near Nordhausen. A starved seventeen-year-old Pole, still wearing his prison uniform, showed Charles the camp's crematorium. Twenty-five thousand people had been cremated in its furnaces in the past year and a half, the young Pole told Charles.

"Here was a place where men and life and death had reached the lowest form of degradation," Charles wrote in his journal. "How could any reward in national progress even faintly justify the establishment and operation of such a place?" But seeing the horrors of Camp Dora did not lead Charles to question his own prewar praise of Germany. Or to retract anything he had said in his America First speeches.

Following his return to the United States, Charles and Anne settled into their first permanent home since Highfields, a nine-bedroom house on the shore of Long Island Sound near Darien, Connecticut. In October 1946 their second daughter, Reeve, was born—the Lindberghs' sixth and last child.

During the late 1940s Cold War tensions mounted between the United States and the Soviet Union. Charles was asked to serve on a committee to reorganize the Strategic Air Command. He made recommendations on pilot training, the location of air bases, and the effectiveness of various weapons systems. An ardent Cold Warrior, he believed that America's only security rested in its ability to retaliate with overwhelming force against any enemy.

Charles had never been satisfied with the hastily written book about his Paris flight, *We*. For over a decade, starting while he was living in Europe, he had been working on another, more detailed account of the journey and what led up to it. Titled *The Spirit of St. Louis*, the book was published at last in 1953. It received enthusiastic reviews, became an immediate best-seller, and was awarded the Pulitzer Prize for biography in 1954.

That same year President Dwight D. Eisenhower, in belated recognition of Charles's wartime services, restored his commission in the reserves and promoted him to brigadier general. Also in 1954 Charles lost one of his staunchest supporters, his mother. Evangeline Lindbergh died in Detroit after a long struggle with Parkinson's disease.

Anne Lindbergh joined her husband on the bestseller list in 1955 when she published *Gift from the Sea*. This meditation on what it meant to be a woman and a wife struck a chord with thousands upon thousands of female book buyers. Once again the Lindberghs were at the center of the nation's attention.

For a change, Charles didn't seem to mind. With a receding hairline,

Lindbergh is sworn in as a brigadier general in the U.S. Air Force Reserve by Secretary of the Air Force Harold E. Talbott, 1954. National Air and Space Museum, Smithsonian Institution.

slight stoop, and somewhat heavier body, he wasn't recognized as often in public these days. And he declined invitations to appear on television, not wanting people to be able to identify and hound him.

As Charles continued to fly, he got an alarming overview of the drastic changes occurring in the natural world. He saw thickly forested areas stripped bare for their lumber, and watched as suburban developments swallowed up all the available open spaces on the outskirts of cities.

These changes affected Charles deeply and led to his joining in efforts to preserve the environment. Starting in the mid-1960s he became an active supporter of the World Wildlife Fund. "Where civilization is most advanced, few birds exist," he wrote in an article for *Reader's Digest*. "I realized that if I had to choose, I would rather have birds than airplanes."

Charles traveled all over the world in an attempt to save endangered species. He flew to Peru to see that country's president and request protection for the humpback and blue whales that Peruvian whalers were harpooning. He journeyed to Alaska to urge the state legislature to repeal the bounty on wolves. Wherever he went, his fame as an aviator and his obvious concern for wildlife made people listen to what he had to say.

Besides their home in Connecticut, the Lindberghs now had two other residences. Anne had bought a chalet overlooking Lake Geneva in Switzerland, and they usually spent the summer there. Charles had built a cottage on Maui in the Hawaiian Islands—"my favorite place in all the world," he said. He and Anne stayed in the cottage during January and February, returning to Connecticut in the spring. By this time even their youngest child had grown up and left home.

As the 1960s came to an end Charles was concentrating most of his conservation efforts on Asia and the South Pacific. He flew to Indonesia to persuade President Sukarno to set up sanctuaries for the Javanese rhinoceros. In the Philippines he convinced President Ferdinand Marcos to establish a preserve for the tamarau, a rare kind of wild buffalo.

When Charles heard that a small tribe living a Stone Age existence had been discovered on one of the Philippine Islands, he joined the first expedition to visit them. The tribe, called the Tasaday, lived in caves in a remote jungle region and survived on a diet of fruit, roots, and tadpoles. They had no weapons, and no words in their language for "war" or "enemy."

To reach the Tasaday Charles and the other members of the expedition flew to the site of the tribe's caves by helicopter. Then they leaped onto a rickety wooden platform that had been constructed at treetop level and climbed down a rope ladder to the jungle floor below. It

Charles gives a Tasaday child a piggyback ride in the Philippines, 1971. National Air and Space Museum, Smithsonian Institution.

reminded Charles of his days as a barnstormer, when he would walk out on the plane's wing and make a double parachute jump.

The Tasaday called Lindbergh Kakay Shalo (meaning "friend Charles") and served him one of their favorite foods—brown grubs gathered from the bottoms of rotting logs. Charles not only swallowed the grubs but smiled and said they tasted a little like oysters.

In one sense Lindbergh regretted that the Tasaday had been exposed to twentieth-century civilization. "Now there's no turning back," he said. But, he added, "great care can be taken to see that the Tasaday are not destroyed or allowed to destroy themselves." A few weeks later—partly as a result of Lindbergh's special pleading—President Marcos created a reserve of more than 42,000 acres for the Tasaday and their closest neighbors.

Charles rarely got tired, but in 1972 he began to feel more and more fatigued. He postponed or canceled several foreign trips, saying he had a bad case of shingles. Actually, his doctors had discovered during a routine checkup that he was suffering from lymphatic cancer. They thought there was a good chance of recovery, but within a year the cancer had spread.

When the doctors told Charles he had at most a few more months to live, he decided to return to his beloved cottage on Maui to die. During his last weeks he planned his funeral service and burial with the same meticulous care he had given to preparations for the Paris flight. He died at the age of seventy-two on August 26, 1974, with his wife, Anne, and son Land at his bedside.

Today hundreds of visitors each week find their way to Charles Lindbergh's grave. They ride in tour buses or private cars along a narrow, winding road that leads to the gravesite on a hill overlooking the blue Pacific. Even in death, and even in this remote location, Charles Lindbergh has not been able to escape the gaze of the curious.

The oldest visitors probably remember where they were on the day of Lindbergh's historic flight. Middle-aged men and women may recall that he was accused of being a Nazi sympathizer during World War II.

Charles Lindbergh at age sixty-nine, in 1971. Photo by John Ferguson, the Minnesota Historical Society.

Chances are many of the youngest visitors have no idea who Lindbergh was or what he did that made him famous.

Looking back over his life, one has to acknowledge that Charles Lindbergh's record was a mixed one. His acceptance of a medal from Adolf Hitler now seems even more naive than it did to critics in the 1930s. And his prewar speeches on behalf of isolationism sound at best ill-advised, at worst downright destructive.

That's not to minimize or deny the remarkable skills he displayed over and over again as an aviator. From his days as an airmail pilot through his mapping the first transpacific and transatlantic air routes with Anne, he proved himself a genuine pioneer.

Above all, though, Charles Lindbergh should be remembered for his almost incredible solo flight to France in 1927. It was one of the great adventures of the twentieth century. And it earned Charles—Lucky Lindy, the Lone Eagle—an enduring reputation as one of the century's greatest heroes.

Not a Superman, as the media of the time often portrayed him, but an all-too-human hero. A man with more than his share of weaknesses, along with tremendous strengths.

Important Dates in Charles A. Lindbergh's Life

February 4, 1902—Charles Lindbergh is born in Detroit, Michigan.

September, 1920—Enrolls as a freshman at the University of Wisconsin in Madison.

March, 1922—Leaves the University to enter a flying school in Lincoln, Nebraska.

April, 1922—Goes up in a plane for the first time.

Summer and fall, 1922—Barnstorms in the Middle West as a mechanic, wing-walker, and parachute jumper.

April, 1923—Buys his own plane and goes up on his first solo flight.

Summer, 1923—Barnstorms on his own in the Middle West.

March 15, 1924—Enters an Army Air Service training school in San Antonio, Texas, as a cadet.

May 24, 1924—Father, C. A. Lindbergh, dies.

March, 1925—Graduates with honors from the training school and is commissioned a second lieutenant in the Air Service Reserve Corps.

April, 1926—Becomes an airmail pilot and flies the first airmail from St. Louis to Chicago.

Fall, 1926—Dreams of being the first pilot to fly nonstop from New York to Paris.

Winter and spring, 1926–27—Works to make his dream a reality by seeking backers for such a flight and looking for the right plane.

March–May, 1927—Supervises the design and construction of the *Spirit of St. Louis* in San Diego, and flies it cross-country to Long Island, New York.

May 20–21, 1927—Flies nonstop across the Atlantic Ocean from Roosevelt Field, Long Island, to Le Bourget Airport, Paris.

May–June, 1927—Receives ecstatic welcomes in Paris, Brussels, and London.

June 11, 1927—Returns home to Washington and is presented with the Distinguished Flying Cross by President Calvin Coolidge.

June–July, 1927—Writes *We*, an account of his historic flight.

July–December, 1927—Makes a nationwide tour in the *Spirit of St. Louis* to promote aviation.

December, 1927—Meets Anne Morrow in Mexico City while on a goodwill trip to Mexico and Latin America.

May 27, 1929—Marries Anne Morrow at her parents' home in Englewood, New Jersey.

1929–30—Teaches Anne to fly, and together they break the speed record for a flight from Los Angeles to New York in the spring of 1930.

June 22, 1930—Anne gives birth to the Lindberghs' first child, Charles Jr.

July–October, 1931—The Lindberghs fly to Alaska, Japan, and China to scout possible air routes for Pan American Airlines.

Fall, 1931—Charles and Anne move into their new home near Hopewell, New Jersey.

March 1, 1932—The Lindberghs' little son, Charles Jr., is kidnaped.

April 2, 1932—Through an intermediary, Charles pays a $50,000 ransom for his son to a mystery man with a German accent.

May 12, 1932—The body of Charles Jr. is discovered in the woods less than two miles from the Lindberghs' home.

August 16, 1932—Anne gives birth to the Lindberghs' second son, Jon.

July–December, 1933—Charles and Anne explore north and south Atlantic air routes for Pan American, and visit eleven European countries.

September 20, 1934—Bruno Richard Hauptmann is arrested in connection with the Lindbergh kidnaping.

January 2, 1935—The trial of Bruno Hauptmann for kidnaping and murder begins in Flemington, New Jersey.

February 13, 1935—Hauptmann is found guilty and is condemned to death.

December, 1935—The Lindberghs and their son Jon move to England to escape continuing harassment by the press.

April 3, 1936—Bruno Hauptmann dies in the electric chair.

July–August, 1936—The Lindberghs visit Nazi Germany and are received by Hermann Göring.

May 12, 1937—The Lindberghs' third son, Land, is born in London.

October, 1937—The Lindberghs make a second trip to Germany.

May, 1938—The Lindberghs and their two sons move to Illiec, an island off the northeast coast of France.

August, 1938—The Lindberghs visit the Soviet Union on a fact-finding mission.

October, 1938—Charles receives a medal from Hermann Göring during a third visit to Germany.

April, 1939—With war looming in Europe, Charles returns to the United States, followed a month later by Anne and the children.

September 1, 1939—Germany invades Poland and World War II begins.

September 15, 1939—Charles speaks out over all three major radio networks against any U.S. involvement in the war.

October, 1939–April, 1941—Through radio talks, speeches, and articles, Charles continues to argue that the United States should maintain an isolationist policy and avoid taking sides in the European war.

October 2, 1940—Anne gives birth to the Lindberghs' first daughter, named Anne, after her mother.

February, 1941—Charles testifies in Congress against the Lend-Lease Bill designed to aid Great Britain in its war effort.

April, 1941—Charles joins the isolationist organization known as America First and gives his first of many talks on its behalf.

September 11, 1941—At an America First rally in Des Moines, Iowa, Charles makes a speech that is denounced on all sides for being antisemitic.

December 7, 1941—Japan mounts a surprise attack on the U.S. naval base at Pearl Harbor in the Hawaiian Islands, bringing America into World War II.

December 8, 1941—In the face of the war, America First cancels all future meetings and rallies.

Late December, 1941—Charles volunteers his services in the Air Corps but is rejected because of his isolationist views.

1941–1945—Charles serves as a consultant to various aircraft companies and makes inspection tours of the South Pacific and postwar Germany.

August 13, 1942—Anne gives birth to the Lindberghs' fourth son, Scott.

October 20, 1946—The Lindberghs' sixth and last child, a daughter, Reeve, is born.

1953–54—Charles's full-scale study of his Paris flight, *The Spirit of St. Louis*, becomes a national bestseller in 1953 and wins the Pulitzer Prize for biography in 1954.

April, 1954—President Dwight D. Eisenhower restores Charles's military commission and promotes him to brigadier general.

September, 1954—Charles's mother, Evangeline, dies of Parkinson's disease.

The 1960s—Charles becomes an active supporter of worldwide conservation efforts.

1971—Charles visits the Tasaday, a tribe living a Stone-Age existence in a remote corner of the Philippine Islands.

August 26, 1974—Charles Lindbergh dies of cancer at the age of seventy-two in his cottage on the Hawaiian island of Maui.

Bibliography and Source Notes

OVERALL

Any biographer of Charles A. Lindbergh would have to begin, as I did, with a study of the man's own autobiographical writings. These include *Boyhood on the Upper Mississippi* (Minnesota Historical Society, 1972), which is filled with anecdotes about his youth; *We* (G. P. Putnam's Sons, 1927), his first account of the history-making Paris flight; *The Spirit of St. Louis* (Charles Scribner's Sons, 1953), the expanded, Pulitzer Prize–winning story of that flight, with autobiographical flashbacks; *The Wartime Journals of Charles A. Lindbergh* (Harcourt Brace Jovanovich, 1970), which details his experiences before, during, and immediately after World War II; and *Autobiography of Values* (Harcourt Brace Jovanovich, 1977), an unfinished manuscript that was published after Lindbergh's death.

For another intimate view of the man, one should dip into the five volumes of diaries and letters compiled by his wife, Anne Morrow Lindbergh. All her books were published by Harcourt Brace Jovanovich. Spanning the years from 1922 to 1944, the five titles are: *Bring Me a Unicorn* (1971), *Hour of Gold, Hour of Lead* (1973), *Locked Rooms and Open Doors* (1974), *The Flower and the Nettle* (1976), and *War Within and Without* (1980).

Of interest, too, are the travel books Anne Morrow Lindbergh wrote about the transpacific and transatlantic flights she made with her husband: *North to the Orient* (1935) and *Listen! The Wind* (1938). Providing additional details on the Atlantic journey is her article "Flying Around the North Atlantic," which appeared in the September 1934 issue of *National Geographic*. Her book *The Wave of the Future* (1940) offers a vivid insight into the Lindberghs' frame of mind at the outset of World War II.

These books by Charles and Anne Lindbergh are, of course, subjective and sometimes limited in their recounting of events. For example, Charles Lindbergh devoted only three pages of his 423-page *Autobiography of Values* to the kidnaping and death of his firstborn son and the trial of Bruno Hauptmann for the crime. And he never mentioned Hauptmann by name.

In order to obtain a more complete picture of Lindbergh's life, one must turn to biographies written by others. The ones I found most revealing and accurate were *The Hero* by Kenneth S. Davis (Doubleday and Company, 1959); *Loss of Eden: A Biography of Charles and Anne Morrow Lindbergh* by Joyce Milton (HarperCollins, 1993); and *The Last Hero: Charles A. Lindbergh* by Walter Sanford Ross (Harper & Row, 1968). Davis is especially good at describing the role the mass media played in shaping Lindbergh's life and career. Milton brings excitement and a grasp of detail to her account of the kidnaping of Charles Lindbergh Jr. and the arrest and trial of Bruno Hauptmann. Ross's knowledge of aviation history complements Lindbergh's own recital of his early days as a flier.

Other books that were particularly useful as I pursued my research were Dorothy Hermann's biography *Anne Morrow Lindbergh: A Gift for Life* (Ticknor & Fields, 1992); George Waller's *Kidnap: The Story of the Lindbergh Case* (The Dial Press, 1961); Harold Nicolson's *Diaries and Letters: 1930–1939*, edited by his son, Nigel Nicolson (Atheneum, 1966); and E. B. White's collection of essays *One Man's Meat* (Harper & Row, 1982).

SOURCE NOTES BY CHAPTER

PROLOGUE: The *Spirit of St. Louis* on display at the National Air and Space Museum in Washington: notes taken by the author during a visit.

CHAPTER 1: The young Lindbergh's sighting of a plane and details of his life on the Little Falls farm: Lindbergh's *The Spirit of St. Louis* and his *Boyhood on the Upper Mississippi*. Personal histories of C.A. and Evangeline Lindbergh: the Davis, Milton, and Ross biographies. Lindbergh's relationship with his grandfather Land: *The Spirit of St. Louis*. The young Lindbergh's driving experiences with the family car: *Boyhood on the Upper Mississippi*. The braking incident in Duluth: Davis.

CHAPTER 2: Impressions of Lindbergh by his high school classmates: interviews with reporters in Little Falls after his Paris flight, as quoted in Davis. Roy Larson's memories of Lindbergh on his motorcycle: Davis. Lindbergh's interest in aviation sparked by World War I air ace story: *Boyhood on the Upper Mississippi*. Father's and mother's reactions to his wanting to learn to fly: *The Spirit of St. Louis*.

CHAPTER 3: Lindbergh's thoughts during his first flight, his early barnstorming days in Nebraska, his double parachute jump, and his western barnstorming tour: *The Spirit of St. Louis*. Convincing his father to back the purchase of his first plane: Davis.

CHAPTER 4: Lindbergh's first solo flight: *The Spirit of St. Louis*. Helping his father campaign, his decision to enlist as an Air Service cadet, and details concerning the final illness and death of C. A. Lindbergh: Davis.

CHAPTER 5: Lindbergh's stunts with the Mil-Hi Flying Circus: Davis. His experiences as an airmail pilot, including his forced parachute jump near Chicago and his first thoughts of flying nonstop to Paris: *The Spirit of St. Louis*.

CHAPTER 6: Information about early attempts to fly the Atlantic, the Orteig Prize, and René Fonck's aborted flight: Davis, Ross. Lindbergh's plans for the trip and his search for backers: *The Spirit of St. Louis*, supplemented by material from Davis, Ross, and Milton.

CHAPTER 7: Designing and building the *Spirit of St. Louis* and flying it across the country: *The Spirit of St. Louis*, Davis, and Ross.

CHAPTER 8: Preparations in New York for the Atlantic flight: *The Spirit of St. Louis*, Davis, Ross, and Milton. Evangeline Lindbergh's dialogue when she visited her son: reports from *The New York Times* and the *New York Herald-Tribune*, as quoted in Davis. Lindbergh's dialogue before he departed: article by Frank Tichenor in *Aero Digest* magazine, as quoted in Davis.

CHAPTER 9: Lindbergh's experiences during the first part of the Paris flight: *The Spirit of St. Louis*. Reactions of the people and press back home: Davis. Lindbergh's means of relieving himself on the plane: a footnote in Milton.

CHAPTER 10: The events that occurred during the second half of the flight, including the appearance of the phantoms: *The Spirit of St. Louis*. Quote from Will Rogers's column: Davis.

CHAPTER 11: Lindbergh's reception in Paris and the advertising and film offers he received: largely from Davis, supplemented by Milton. His welcomes in Brussels and London: Davis. The king of England's personal question: Milton. Other nonstop flights from America to Europe after Lindbergh's: Davis.

CHAPTER 12: Reception in America: Davis, supplemented by Milton.

CHAPTER 13: Lindbergh's visit to Mexico: Davis, supplemented by Milton and Anne Morrow Lindbergh's *Bring Me a Unicorn*. Courtship of Anne Morrow and wedding: Davis, Milton, *Bring Me a Unicorn*, and Lindbergh's *Autobiography of Values*.

CHAPTER 14: The Lindberghs as copilots: Davis, Milton, Anne Morrow Lindbergh's *Hour of Gold, Hour of Lead*. Lindbergh and Dr. Alexis Carrel: Davis, Milton, Ross, *Autobiography of Values*. The Lindberghs' 1931 trip to the Far East: Davis, Milton, Anne Morrow Lindbergh's *North to the Orient*, *Autobiography of Values*.

CHAPTER 15: The kidnaping of Charles Lindbergh Jr.: Milton, Davis, Ross, *Hour of Gold, Hour of Lead*, George Waller's *Kidnap*.

CHAPTER 16: Dr. Condon's role in the case and the payment of the ransom: Milton, Davis, Waller, Ross, *Hour of Gold, Hour of Lead*.

CHAPTER 17: Aftermath of the crime: Milton, Davis, Ross. The Lindberghs' Atlantic and European flights: Davis, Milton, Anne Morrow Lindbergh's article "Flying Around the North Atlantic," and her two books *Listen! The Wind* and *Locked Rooms and Open Doors*. The 1934 airmail controversy: Davis, Ross, Milton, *Autobiography of Values*.

CHAPTER 18: The arrest, trial, and conviction of Bruno Hauptmann: Milton, Waller, Davis, Ross. Harold Nicolson's impressions of Lindbergh: Nicolson's

Diaries and Letters, supplemented by Milton. Lindbergh's decision to move to Europe: Davis, Milton, *Locked Rooms and Open Doors*, *Autobiography of Values*.

CHAPTER 19: Reactions to the Lindberghs' departure: Davis, Milton. The Lindberghs' first and second visits to Germany: Davis, Milton, Anne Morrow Lindbergh's *The Flower and the Nettle*, *Autobiography of Values*. The Lindberghs' move to Illiec: Milton, Davis, *The Flower and the Nettle*.

CHAPTER 20: The Lindberghs' 1938 visit to the Soviet Union: Davis, Milton, Lindbergh's *Wartime Journals*, *The Flower and the Nettle*. The Czech crisis: Davis, Ross. Lindbergh's assessment of German air strength: Davis, *Wartime Journals*. Presentation of German medal to Lindbergh: Davis, Milton, *Wartime Journals*, *Autobiography of Values*, *The Flower and the Nettle*.

CHAPTER 21: Lindbergh's return to America and inspection tours: Davis, *Wartime Journals*. President Roosevelt's offer: Davis biography of Lindbergh, also Davis's *F.D.R.: Into the Storm, 1937–1940* (Random House, 1993). Lindbergh's isolationist speeches: Davis, Milton, *Wartime Journals*, Anne Morrow Lindbergh's *War Within and Without*. E. B. White's comments on *The Wave of the Future*: his collection of essays *One Man's Meat*. Lindbergh's testimony before Congress: Davis, Milton, *Wartime Journals*.

CHAPTER 22: Lindbergh and America First: Davis, Milton, *Wartime Journals*, *Autobiography of Values*, *War Within and Without*. Harold Nicolson's view of Lindbergh's isolationism: article in *The Spectator* of London, October 1939. Lindbergh's statement after Pearl Harbor: Davis.

CHAPTER 23: Lindbergh's wartime consultantships: Davis, Ross, Milton, *Wartime Journals*. Lindbergh's experiences in the Pacific combat zone: Davis, *Wartime Journals*. Lindbergh's reactions to Camp Dora in Germany: *Wartime Journals*. The Lindberghs' activities in the 1950s and 1960s: Milton, Dorothy Hermann's biography *Anne Morrow Lindbergh*. Lindbergh's conservation efforts, his last days, and his death: *Autobiography of Values*, Milton, obituary by Alden Whitman in *The New York Times*, August 27, 1974.

Index

Page numbers in italics refer to photos and/or captions